Advanced and Professional Typewriting

Second Edition

Molly Sedgwick FRSA FSCT

Formerly lecturer in Secretarial Studies Eastbourne College of Further Education

PITMAN PUBLISHING LIMITED
128 Long Acre, London WC2E 9AN

Associated Companies
Pitman Publishing Pty Ltd, Melbourne
Pitman Publishing New Zealand Ltd, Wellington

First published in Great Britain 1972
Second Edition 1985

British Library Cataloguing in Publication Data
Sedgwick, Molly
Advanced and professional typewriting – 2nd ed.
1. Typewriting
I. Title
652.3 Z49

Text set in IBM Press Roman
Printed and bound in Great Britain
at The Bath Press, Bath

ISBN 0 273 01933 3

Pitman

Task 111 (continued)

(5) The Vendors who have not made any previous conveyance or assent in respect of a legal estate in the property hereinafter described have agreed with the Purchaser for the sale thereof to her for an estate in fee simple in possession free from incumbrances at the price of eighty thousand five hundred pounds (£80,500) caps

NOW THIS DEED WITNESSETH as follows:-

1. IN pursuance of the said agreement & in consideration of the sum of eighty thousand five hundred pounds (£80,500) to the Vendors now paid by the Purchaser (the receipt of which sum the Vendors hereby acknowledge) the vendors u/c as Personal Representatives of the Testator & in exercise of their statutory powers in this behalf & of all other powers them enabling hereby convey unto the Purchaser FIRST ALL THAT piece of land comprising One acre or thereabouts together with the dwellinghouse & premises erected thereon or on some part thereof known as Downsview situate at Salturn in the County of Sussex & coloured pink on the plan endorsed on a Conveyance dated the Twenty-third day of November One thousand nine hundred & thirty-six & made between Mary Nowne of the first part Oscar Ping of the second part & the Testator of the 3rd part AND SECONDLY ALL THAT piece or parcel of land situate adjoining to the north side of the property hereinbefore described & being 133 ft in length & 14 ft in width & coloured green on the said plan which said plan is for the purposes of identification only TO HOLD the same unto the purchaser in fee simple u.c

2. THE Vendors hereby acknowledge the right of the Purchaser to production of the Probate of the Will of the Testator & to delivery of copies thereof

sp. caps IN WITNESS whereof the parties hereto have hereunto set their hands & seals the day & yr. first before written

SIGNED SEALED AND DELIVERED by the said ANTHONY BERTRAM CROTCHETT in the presence of:

SIGNED SEALED AND DELIVERED by the said DAVID EDWARD FRENCH in the presence of:

TYPIST This Conveyance is ready for engrossing please ensure that consistency is maintained throughout & mark in pencil where each separatory is to go

Publisher's Preface

This second edition has been extensively rewritten and brought up to date by Molly Sedgwick, a very successful teacher of typewriting, many of whose students have been among medal-winners in public examinations.

International paper sizes and the 24-hour clock are used throughout. Whilst the book is presented on 253 x 203 mm paper size for convenience in handling, all tasks have been prepared with the international paper sizes (A4 and A5) in mind, and for pica and elite typewriter pitch.

The author presents up-to-date, lively and useful material. All the information is intended to assist the student as well as office personnel. Much research has been undertaken and the new layouts have all been checked and verified for authenticity and accuracy in modern display.

Advanced and Professional Typewriting is intended to meet the needs of all students in schools, colleges, secretarial bureaux and agencies, Government departments, training schools within industry, H.M. Services and business offices throughout the English-speaking world. It is also for teachers wishing to raise their students to a high professional level, and it is a mine of information for those people preparing for the Royal Society of Arts Teacher's Certificate in Typewriting, and the Pitman Typewriting Teacher's Diploma of the Joint Examining Board. The dual purpose of theory for the intermediate, and practice for the advanced students is evident throughout.

The author and publishers wish to acknowledge with sincere appreciation the help that they have received from many professional and examining bodies; and from the author's working colleagues. In particular, the author wishes her thanks to be expressed to the Pitman staff for checking and collating the script.

Thanks are due to the following for permission to reproduce extracts from the works mentioned:

The Beauty of England by Thomas Burke—George Harrap & Company Ltd.
The Kon-Tiki Expedition by Thor Heyerdahl—George Allen & Unwin Ltd.
High Endeavour by Edward Seago—Collins Ltd.
The Overloaded Ark by Gerald M. Durrell—Faber and Faber Ltd.
When the Chute Went Up by Dolly Shepherd—Robert Hale Ltd.

Note: The telephone numbers, names, addresses and postcodes in this book are intended to be fictitious.

T H I S C O N V E Y A N C E is made the ⋏ (insert)

day of One thousand nine hundred and

B E T W E E N ANTHONY BERTRAM CROTCHETT of Tree Tops 123 Branch Street Blighton in the County of Sussex Bank Manager and DAVID EDWARD FRENCH of 99 Melk Street Blighton in the said County of Sussex Solicitor (hereinafter called "the Vendors") of the one part and GEORGINA SARAH INCHAM of 17c The Pitts Bromley in the County of Kent Widow (hereinafter called "the Purchaser") of the other part

W H E R E A S

(1) John Kenneth Loe (hereinafter called "the Testator") late of Two Beeches Ravencroft Road Worthington in the County of Sussex Gentleman by his Will dated the Twenty-fifth day of May One thousand nine hundred and sixty appointed Bartons Bank and the Vendors to be the Executors and Trustees thereof

(2) The Testator executed two Codicils to his said Will which did not affect the appointment of Executors and Trustees thereof

(3) The Testator died on the Fifth day of September One thousand nine hundred and eighty-one and Probate of his said Will was granted out of the Blighton District Probate Registry to the Executors therein named on the Fourth day of February One thousand nine hundred and eighty-two

(4) The Testator was at the date of his death seized of the property hereinafter described for an estate in fee simple in possession free from incumbrances

(continued)

Contents

Task 110

Miss Y. This is so straightforward we can engross straight away

Please type an ~~draft~~ engrossment of the following will to be sent to Mr. Doe –

I JOHN DOE of 56 Tumbledown Green, Reading in the County of Berkshire HEREBY REVOKE all former Wills & Testamentary dispositions heretofore made by me AND DECLARE this to be my last Will

1. I APPOINT RICHARD ROE of 8c Roundabout Crescent Guildford in the County of Surrey to be the EXECUTOR and TRUSTEE of this my Will

2. I BEQUEATH the following pecuniary legacies:-

TO/ a) TO my brother Jack Doe the sum of ~~FIVE HUNDRED~~ ONE THOUSAND POUNDS (~~£500~~) (£1000)

b) TO my friend Richard Black of Tom Thumb Cottage Tumbledown Green Reading the sum of FIVE HUNDRED POUNDS (£500)

3 I GIVE DEVISE and BEQUEATH all my Estate both real and personal whatsoever & wheresoever situate not hereby or by any Codicil hereto otherwise specifically disposed of unto my Trustee UPON TRUST after the payment thereout of all my just debts & testamentary & funeral expenses (uc/) for such of my sisters Amy Bee & Dee Gee (Joy Bee) of 59c Honey Drive Manchester as shall be living at my death and if more than one in equal shares Absolutely

IN WITNESS whereof I have hereunto set my hand this day of One thousand nine hundred and

SIGNED by the above named Testator JOHN DOE as and for his last Will in the presence of us both being present at the same time who at his request in his presence and in the presence of each other have hereunto subscribed our names as witnesses:- } X

1

2

Miss Young

Put pencilled cross where signatory is to sign & in place of 1 & 2 pencil in name, address, occupation (under each other) to indicate to the witnesses where they have to sign.

Index

References in italic type are to pages on which the tasks or drills appear.

Task 109

THIS ASSENT is made the day of One thousand nine hundred & BETWEEN JESSIE DOE of 13a Watchtower Road Cheltenham in the County of Gloucester & JOHN DOE of 17c Appledore Rd Cheltenham in the said County of Gloucester of the one part

caps & Roberta Roe of Highfield, Rowena Lane, Ipswich in the County of Suffolk of the other part.

sc/ WHEREAS:-

1. Richard Roe (hereinafter called "the Testator") died on the fifth day of May One thousand nine hundred & sixty-six & his will uc/ was proved in the Principal Probate Registry by Douglas Robert & Doe

eight/ on the Fourteenth day of June One thousand nine hundred & seventy

2. THE said Douglas Robert Doe died on the Seventh day of June one thousand nine hundred & seventy-one without having completed the administration of the Testator's Estate & his Will was proved in the Principal Probate Registry on the ~~Twel~~ Twentieth day of February One thousand nine hundred & seventy-two by the said Jessie Doe & the said John Doe

uc/ 3. BY his said Will the Testator gave all his estate jointly to Anne Beatrice Roe & the said Roberta Roe.

4. THE said Anne Beatrice Roe died on the seventeenth day of uc/ March One thousand nine hundred & eighty-four & by her Will appointed the said Roberta Roe the sole beneficiary & one of the Executors thereof & the said Roberta Roe proved the said Will of the said Anne Beatrice Roe in the Principal Probate Registry on the Sixth day of June One thousand nine hundred & eighty-five Robert Thomas Brown having renounced Probate thereof

NOW WE the said Jessie Doe & the said John Doe

uc/ hereby as Personal representatives of the Testator ASSENT

uc/ to the vesting in the said Roberta Roe of all That the Freehold premises known as & situate at Highfield Rowena Lane Ipswich in the County of Suffolk for an estate in fee simple

AND WE HEREBY ACKNOWLEDGE the right of the said Roberta Roe to the production of the Probates of the Wills of the Testator & of the said Douglas Robert Doe & to delivery of copies thereof

AS WITNESS the hands of the said Jessie Doe & the said John Doe the day & year first above written

SIGNED by the said JESSIE DOE in the presence of:- }

SIGNED by the said JOHN DOE in the presence of:- }

Endorse please ready to send to Ross & Pinchen of Ipswich.

the building of which the demised premises form part and all other persons entitled thereto

(i) the right of ingress to and egress from all other portions of the said building over and along all the usual entrances and passageways leading thereto from and over any part of the demised premises

(ii) the right of free passage and running of water and soil in and through the sewers and drains through or under the demised premises

TO HOLD the demised premises unto the Tenant from the twenty-fifth day of March One thousand nine hundred and

(Insert) ⋏ for the term of Twenty-one years Paying therefor the yearly rent of Two thousand pounds (£2000) by equal quarterly payments on the usual quarter days in every year the first of such payments to be made on the Twenty-fifth day of March One thousand nine hundred and ⋏ (Insert as above)

IN WITNESS whereof the parties hereto have hereunto set their hands and seals the day and year first before written

SIGNED SEALED AND DELIVERED)
by the said JOHN ANDREW)
BLACK in the presence of:)

This Lease is made the

day of One

thousand nine hundred and BETWEEN

JOHN ANDREW BLACK of 6 Roach Road, Hastings, in the County of Sussex Accountant (hereinafter called "the Lessor" which expression shall where the context so admits include the person for the time being entitled to the reversion immediately expectant on the term hereby created) of the one part and JAMES DOUGLAS SMITH and GEORGE ROBERT SMITH both of 8 The Crescent, Wimbledon in the County of London Bakers (hereinafter called "the Tenants" which expression shall where the context so admits include their successors in title) of the other part

W I T N E S S E T H as follows:-

1. THE Lessor hereby demises unto the Tenants ALL THAT Southern half of the shop premises on part of the ground floor of the premises known as 320 Broad Street, Wimbledon in the County of London having a frontage of Twelve feet Six inches to Broad Street aforesaid and a return frontage to Trencham Road Together with the use in common or with the Tenant of the Northern half of the said shop premises of the lavatory and Together with all rights of light air and other easements belonging to or hitherto enjoyed by the demised premises Together with the rights to support and shelter from the other parts of the building of which the demised premises form part EXCEPT AND RESERVING to the Lessor and the tenants and occupiers of other portions of

(continued)

Introduction

The modern business world demands speed and efficiency.

Expert typists, in whatever situation they may find themselves, must measure up to these requirements, and therefore their concern is for *accuracy* and *speed* in typing, together with a knowledge of *how* to deal with any work they may be given.

The aim of this book is to build on basic knowledge already acquired and to prepare students, firstly, for advanced typewriting examinations, and secondly, to take their place in the business world.

It is assumed that the student using an advanced typewriting book already possesses the basic theory rules, and has achieved a reasonable speed and degree of accuracy, so that many elementary points will be taken for granted. However, in order to ensure that the student who wishes to become an expert may be aware of the finer details of the theory, a résumé of the most important points will be given with each section.

The structure of this book. As examinations are only the *first* step in the careers of typists or secretaries, the scope of this book is wide, to prepare for practical work in all types of offices. For this reason, the tasks are not only confined to those found in the examination room. Employers vary in their likes and dislikes of different styles of work, and as professional typists must be adaptable, traditional methods of display are given side by side with the modern styles adopted in many offices.

Examination preparation has been carefully considered in the selection of material, especially that required for advanced examinations. As past papers are used so extensively in schools and colleges, it has been decided not to print any particular examination paper.

Plan of presentation. As students preparing for advanced work need a variety of the more difficult typewritten matter, the teacher is naturally selective and spends much time in research. For this reason, to locate any given tasks quickly, it has been decided to group the tasks under their various headings. It is not proposed, of course, that students should 'work through' these tasks in the order given, but the teacher should select the tasks from each group as they fit in with her own syllabus.

Accuracy and speed being so essential to first-class work, a number of drills are given at the beginning of the book, to be used either as class work, or individually by students when time permits. Concentration and attention to manipulative techniques are needed to ensure that the adage 'practice makes perfect' is true.

Punctuation—or the incorrect use of it—is the cause of many a failure to an otherwise good typist. The tasks given will assist students, both in copying from correctly punctuated matter, and in providing the opportunity of showing their skill in this vital sphere of typewriting.

Legal definitions

Abstract of Title. A summary of the documents and facts constituting the title to land going back for a minimum period of 15 years, containing copies or abstracts of the documents in a specialised shortened form.

Affidavit. A written statement of facts for use in court proceedings made on oath before a Commissioner for Oaths. A Statutory Declaration is a similar document for use where court proceedings are not involved, and has the same legal effect and is taken before a Commissioner, though it is not on oath.

Agreement. Any document in writing signed by two or more persons agreeing to do something, such as to sell and buy a house.

Brief. The document prepared by a solicitor instructing counsel to appear in court, and containing details of the facts, evidence and documents constituting his client's case. Similar documents prepared by solicitors to instruct counsel to advise or draft documents are called 'Instructions'.

Conveyance. The document by which the vendor of land transfers the legal ownership in it to the purchaser.

Deed. Any document under seal, eg conveyances, mortgages, etc.

Document Under Hand. Any document in writing signed by the parties thereto but not bearing seals, eg most agreements to buy and sell land, and tenancy agreements for periods of three years or less.

Document Under Seal. A deed; a document not only signed by the parties concerned, but also bearing their seals. Companies and corporations have a much larger seal, called a Common Seal, which is affixed to documents and countersigned by one or more individuals as authorised by the company, usually a Director and the Secretary. It is usual now to have a small red circular paper seal affixed to documents, and LS (locus sigilli – the place of the seal) typed on the draft to indicate the seal. Similarly, it is the practice to 'crimp' a Company seal on the outside edge of the document (ie squeeze the pages between the embossed plates of the seal to leave its impression on the pages).

Execute. To execute a document means to sign and seal it in the case of a deed, or to sign it in the case of a will or agreement in writing.

Lease. A contract in writing for a period of three years or more, under seal, whereby one person (the landlord) agrees to let land or premises to another person (the tenant) for a specified period at a certain rent. Leases for three years or less are usually under hand only and are called Tenancy Agreements.

Lessor – the one who grants the lease.
Lessee – the one who is granted the lease.

Probate. This is the procedure by which a Will is put into effect when a testator dies, and is called proving a Will. The executors deliver the original Will, together with an account of the estate and an oath that they will duly administer the estate to the Probate Registry, which issues in exchange, a photostat copy of the Will, bound up with an order of the court under its seal, stating that the Will has been duly proved by the executors. This document is known as a Probate.

In the case of intestacy, a similar procedure is followed except that there is no Will and the document issued by the Registry is called Letters of Administration instead of Probate.

Statement of Claim. The formal document in a High Court action in which the plaintiff sets out the facts on which he relies to support his case and the nature of his claim.

Will. A document in writing containing the express wishes of a person for the distribution of his property and administration of his estate, to take effect on his death.

In England (except in the case of a testator on actual military service) a Will must be in writing and signed at the foot or end thereof by the testator and by two witnesses, both of whom must be present when the testator signs, and both of whom must sign in the presence of the testator.

Note 1. There is a special Attestation Clause applicable only to a Will (*see* page 166).

Note 2. A paper clip should never be put on a Will as the mark will show and difficulty may arise in proving to probate that there was not another portion of the Will attached.

Testator – One who bequeaths property, etc by Will.
Testatrix – Female testator.
Executor – Person appointed by testator to execute his Will.
Executrix – Female executor.

To the Student

Before you begin

You are now on your way to becoming a professional typist, and in the last resort it rests with you whether or not you achieve this goal.

Here are a few points for you to remember when doing any kind of typewritten work:

Correct posture. In order to be in complete control of your machine it is essential to sit correctly, at right angles to the desk, with feet on the floor (or foot rest). Be careful that your wrists neither drop nor are arched.

Quality of touch. With an electronic typewriter or a word processor the final typescript, or printout, is always of a high quality—as it should be when an electric or a manual machine is used. Perfect rhythm is essential, and a uniform rate of typing overall will produce the best results, ensuring that your work has a clear, even appearance.

Accuracy and speed. Speed is useless without accuracy. To acquire both of these, concentration and constant practice are needed.

Repetition practice. Use warming up exercises, drills and alphabetic sentences whenever you can. Concentration on what you are doing is essential. Idle copying has no real value. Be critical of your own work, analyse the kinds of errors you are making and then do remedial exercises to cure your weaknesses.

Economy of movement. Practice on all parts of the typewriter is necessary, until you can use with speed: the carriage return, back spacer, margin release, tabulator keys, shift keys and the top row of keys.

English. In all communications a plain, straightforward style is always preferable to long complicated words and sentences. The grammar should be correct without appearing affected.

Punctuation. This aspect of English cannot be separated from typing, therefore rules should be known and examples studied. The tasks in this book will give you plenty of practice to improve your ability in this field.

Erasures. If erasures are made they should be undetectable. Practise erasing—not in your daily work, but on a practice sheet. Do remember to move your carriage to the side so that rubber dust does not fall into the machine (see pages 25-6).

Tasks. Before beginning to type any task, run through in your mind all the points of theory connected with it as a revision. Read the theory notes and then read any instructions given *very carefully*. Always be sure you know exactly what is required of you before you begin to type.

Presentation of work. When you have completed each piece of work you should look at it critically, considering whether it really is first-class, aesthetic to the eye and of a high standard generally. Proof of the expert typist is that any *obvious* errors or 'slips' in the chief's drafts should automatically be corrected. Bear this in mind when typing the following tasks.

If your typescript is accurate, clean and crisp (with no visible erasures) and has been typed with an even touch, then you can be proud of your efforts and pass on to the next piece of work.

Testimonium and Attestation clauses

Most legal documents end with these two clauses, which are concerned with signing and witnessing, and without which the documents would not be valid. There is a special Attestation Clause applicable only to a Will (*see* page 166) and the witnesses must not be beneficiaries.

Testimonium Clause

This varies according to whether it is under seal or under hand (*see* page 162). It is the clause at the end of a legal document which begins 'IN WITNESS. . .' (if under seal) or 'AS WITNESS . . .' (if under hand).

Attestation Clause

This follows the Testimonium Clause, is typed in single or double spacing, starting at about $\frac{3}{4}$ in. into the left-hand margin, and blocked. Like the Testimonium Clause, it varies according to whether the document is under seal or not.

It is *against* the Attestation Clause that the signatory signs, and *below* which the witnesses sign, giving their address and occupation. *Note*: It is the signature and/or sealing only which is attested.

Examples of a Testimonium and Attestation Clause under seal and under hand respectively are given opposite:

IN WITNESS whereof the parties hereto have hereunto set their hands and seals the day and year first above mentioned

SIGNED SEALED AND DELIVERED)
by the said JOHN DOE in the) (John Doe signs here) (L.S.)
presence of:-)
(witnesses sign here)

THE COMMON SEAL of RICHARD ROE)
& COMPANY LIMITED was hereunto) (L.S.)
affixed in the presence of:-)

(signature here) Director
(" ") Secretary

A S W I T N E S S the hands of the parties hereto the day and year first before written

SIGNED by the said)
JOHN DOE in the) (John Doe signs here)
presence of:-)
(witnesses sign here)

Endorsement

This illustration shows how a legal document should be folded and endorsed in its final form.

1 Typewriter Manipulation Practice

Drill 1

Every word begins and ends on a home key. Type each sentence several times before passing on to the next.

Several students achieved success as accountants.

All shrewd authors seek alliteration's artful aid.

Attend all school lectures and find final success.

Delicious fruits grow in the climate of Australia.

All ambitious students find shorthand advantageous.

A distinguished Swiss addressed delighted listeners.

April sends joyful songsters and delightful flowers.

Foreigners find Londoners stolid and self-satisfied.

Several famous footballers signed forms and departed.

Lord Ammanford addressed several Liberal Associations.

Several aeroplanes and automobiles arrived as ordered.

Foxes steal ducks; lads apples, and dogs small scraps.

Australia supplies apples, apricots, and luscious fruits.

Settlers abound and amass fortunes around diamond fields.

Distinguished aviators accomplished splendid aerial feats.

Douglas fell downstairs, and died several days afterwards.

Fred joined several friends and journeyed across Australia.

Shorthand students should often attend seminars or lectures.

Several legal documents, such as contracts, had disappeared.

Distribution copies of documents

1 **Duplicate documents**. These are two or more identical documents, each signed by all the parties. The endorsement should contain the word 'Duplicate' on all but one copy, which is deemed to be the original.
2 **Counterpart**. This is a duplicate of the original document in every respect except the Attestation Clause, one party signing the original and the other the Counterpart. A document frequently prepared in this way is a Lease. The word Counterpart should be typed on the endorsement.
3 **Certified copies**. These are frequently required and are normally photocopies of executed stamped documents. They are certified thus: 'I/We certify this to be a true copy of the original' and signed by a solicitor. These words may be placed where it is convenient.
4 **Made-up copies**. These are usually uncertified photocopies, sometimes spare carbon copies made to agree with the engrossment, showing (in capitals) the exact form of the signatures of the parties and details of the attesting witnesses. If the document is under seal, it is customary to type 'L.S.' (locus sigilli) against the signature of each party.

General points governing the typing of legal work

1 A *brief* typewriter is desirable, as brief paper (16 in. by 13 in.) is still used in some offices, particularly where accounts are involved.

2 Usually a good quality black record ribbon is used. A ribbon change in mid-document is intolerable. A faint ribbon does not photo-copy clearly.

3 If *specially ruled paper* indicating the margins is not used, margins would be $1\frac{1}{2}$ in. to 2 in. on the left (allowing for the stitching margin), and $\frac{1}{2}$ in. on the right. If both sides of the paper are used, the margins on the even-numbered pages must be sufficiently wide to avoid words being obliterated when the pages are fastened together.

4 An uneven right-hand margin should be avoided, so that, if necessary, words may be hyphenated in the usual way (though this practice is often discouraged).

Short lines are usually filled in with a red line to prevent any possible fraudulent additions.

5 *Erasures* are most undesirable. They waste time and spoil the appearance of the document. They are not fatal to the document, unless obvious, when all parties concerned would have to initial the correction.

6 *No punctuation* is used, except at the end of a Clause in order to avoid ambiguity. Three spaces are left at the end of sentences, however, and a new sentence begins with a capital letter.

7 Drafts are usually numbered, at the bottom or the top of the page, as they consist of separate sheets, but Engrossments are very rarely numbered as these are on double parchment sheets.

8 It is customary to write numbers, including dates, in full, and sums of money also in figures, in brackets, but much depends upon the wishes of the draughtsman. House numbers remain as figures. In documents for use in the High Court and County Courts, particularly Affidavits, it is standard practice to render figures as figures and not in words. If this instruction is not adhered to, the document could be rejected.

9 *Capitalisation* is largely a matter of tradition, designed to highlight the names of the parties, the effect of the document and certain more important features. The following points should be noted.
It is usual to capitalise:–

a The first word/s of the document, indicating the nature of the document, such as THIS AGREEMENT (often in spaced capitals).
b The names of the parties, when *first* mentioned.
c The first word of each recital and each numbered clause, but not when that word is a proper name.
d Such words as BETWEEN, WHEREAS, AND, in certain circumstances. The typist would not be expected to know when to capitalise in these cases, but should follow the indications given by the draughtsman.
e The words of the Testimonium Clause, beginning IN WITNESS . . . or AS WITNESS . . .
f The principal words and the names of the signatories in the Attestation Clause.

Note. When typing capitals and spaced capitals it is important to be consistent in the method of spacing before and after words or groups of words

10 It is necessary to avoid ending the last clause of a document (particularly a Will) on one page and commencing the Attestation Clause on the next page. If a gap is inevitable, it should be ruled through.

11 As Company seals cannot easily reach the centre of an Engrossment, where possible, Attestation Clauses for Companies should take this into account.

Drill 2

Repetitive sentences for speed.	Strokes
Treat life as you want it to treat you.	39
Pinch yourself and know how others feel.	40
The ancestor of every action is a thought.	42
Beware of a sudden friend or a slow enemy.	42
Plan for more than you can do, then do it.	42
Doing nothing is equivalent to doing wrong.	43
Habits are at first cobwebs, at last cables.	44
To talk easily is the great charm of talking.	45
Many a sharp retort is made in blunt language.	45
Trusting a man helps to make him trustworthy.	46
The biggest fool is the man who fools himself.	46
No service degrades which can better our race.	46
Anything that makes a noise satisfies a crowd.	46
We usually dislike things we do not understand.	47
Opportunity is kind, but only to the industrious.	49
Service is the rent we pay for our room on earth.	49

Drill 3

Longer repetitive sentences for speed.	
Bad writing may be a sign of genius but not of wisdom.	54
The art of pleasing is the art of rising in the world.	54
A man's mind should be like a good hotel - always open.	55
Silence is golden when you cannot think of a good answer.	57
A coward dies a thousand deaths, a brave man dies but once.	59

15 Legal Work

The typist who enters a solicitor's office will be given guidance on styles of display and shown examples of documents likely to be required, but she should have a general interest in legal matters and, above all, be able to type accurately and display well. Much of the work may be routine correspondence; a knowledge of legal terminology would be an advantage, but this will be acquired by experience.

The laborious copy-typing of long legal documents has largely been abolished with the advent of the word processor, which has revolutionised legal offices. However, it is still necessary to know the general conventions and displays applying to the preparation of the more common types of legal documents that might be encountered. In all cases display and capitalisation should be followed and any doubtful passages queried, as the typist is not expected to know the intricacies of the law.

1 **The Draft.** This is the document drawn up in the form which satisfies the instructions given by both parties. It is usually prepared in three copies, so that two copies may be sent to the 'opposing' solicitor, and one copy retained. The top copy is then returned 'approved as drawn', or amended in red ink. Subsequent amendments are made in green, violet (or blue), brown, and yellow ink. This ensures that the order of the amendments can be followed. The copy retained in the hands of each solicitor (whilst the top copy 'travels') should be made up with amendments, as the 'travelling' copy is received.

The Draft should be typed in double or treble spacing, and dates, sums of money, etc. should be in words or figures or both, according to the manner in which they will appear in the engrossment. Abbreviations are not used in Draft documents. The endorsement (see illustration) should contain the word 'Draft', and at the foot, the name and address of the solicitor who prepared the Draft. The date at the beginning of a document (and on the endorsement) is left blank, and is added (in ink) at the time of signing the Engrossment.

2 **The Engrossment.** This is the document in its agreed final form. The size and type of paper used, and depth of line spacing, vary according to the wishes of the preparer of the document, although it is customary to type documents expected to have a long life (eg Conveyances, Leases for long terms, Trust documents) on paper parchment. Double spacing is generally used. It is customary to rule the document in an accepted manner, preferably in red ink.

The last page should be left blank for the endorsement. If this is not possible, an extra page should be added at the end of the document.

It should be noted that a well typed, well drawn and neatly sewn document is one of the few advertisements in which a solicitor may indulge.

3 **Endorsement.** This contains the details and description of the document; inaccurate or incomplete endorsements can be a source of considerable error and annoyance, and therefore should contain, in the following order:—

a The date of signing the document.
b The names of the parties.
c The description of the document, completely and neatly summarizing the contents.

On a conveyance or lease this will consist of the property to which it relates. If an agreement of partnership, it will give the summarized legal effect of the document.

The name and address of the firm of solicitors may be typed at the foot of the endorsement, each line centred.

2 **Folding the document.** The endorsement is always typed so that it will be positioned on the outside of a document (each item centred) after it has been folded—either in two lengthways (vertically) with the crease on the left, or into four (horizontally). In the latter case, the document (with the first page uppermost) should be folded from the bottom to the top, and creased carefully, then again folded from the bottom to the top and creased. Holding the bottom crease in the left hand the document is then turned so that the crease is on the left. (*See* example on page 161.)

Drill 3 (*continued*)

	Strokes
He who mixes with his fellows is ever on a voyage of discovery.	63
The barriers are not yet erected that shut out aspiring talent.	63
Let pleasure be ever so innocent, the excess is always criminal.	64
Think as though success were certain, work as though it were not.	65

Drill 4

Each of the following sentences contains all the letters of the alphabet. Type each sentence several times.

	Strokes
The crazy pavement was quickly fixed by a jolly old gardener.	61
Jackman was gazing fixedly over a big hedge in a picturesque lane.	66
The amazing exploits of chivalrous knights will unquestionably afford joy.	74
The firm quickly realized that expenditure on the building was very injudicious.	80
Keen judges told me that antiques of exceptional value were on sale at the charity bazaar.	90
The junior office boy acquired great dexterity and very soon his quickness was perfectly amazing.	97
Existing difficulties may be quickly overcome by courage and zeal, but will be prevented by judicious foresight.	112
Explorers and conquerors alike win fame and join in bringing glory to their countries by their amazing achievements.	116
To reach the zenith of your desires, you must be both just and diligent, and exercise quiet perseverance in your work.	118
Youth's zeal is quickly coaxed into paths of usefulness and service by commercial education, joining wisdom with method.	120

Task 107

Typist Please type the following estimate & specification on headed paper with Quotation immediately under it, in spaced caps & underlined. To go to: J. N. Bristow, 14 Newton Rd., Bournemouth, BH6 5BP.

Dear Sirs — Solent View, Alexander Close

Further to our recent report on the condition of the electrical installations at the above premises, we have pleasure in submitting our estimate for completely re-wiring the installations according to the following details:

SPECIFICATION

(Caps) New wiring to be carried out in P.V.C insulated & sheathed cables concealed where pos. within the building structure, & all in accordance

u.c. with the most recent Institute of electrical engineers' regulations.

NP [All wiring accessories, switches, sockets, ceiling roses & lampholders to be replaced with new. Existing lighting fittings will be re-fixed & connected.

Switches will be of ivory flush pattern, & mounted on surface pattresses where necessary.

Sockets to be 13 amp, wired on Ring main system, ivory in colour, flush or surface mounted as appropriate

SCHEDULE OF ELECTRICAL POINTS: As attached.

Estimated cost, re-wiring only as detailed	£2.400
Contingency sum to allow for cost of carpenter's work in taking up & re-laying floors	500
Contingency sum to allow for taking up & re-laying carpeting by Specialist	150
Contingency sum to allow for making good by painter	120
TOTAL COST	£3,170

(we anticipate) The total given is an outside figure, as in each case the actual cost is likely to be less than the amounts quoted.

We look forward to hearing further from you.

Yf

A J Webster Ltd (Caps)

Estimator

NOTE: The whole of the "specification" incl. total cost to be inset & blocked

Can you use your typewriter efficiently?

Drills for the speedy use of the typewriter. Measurements refer to pica type, elite is shown in brackets.

Carriage Return Drill 5

Set margin at 13 (20). Type the first column straight down the page, returning the carriage as quickly as possible, and continuing to type without a break. Reset your margin at 33 (42) and type as for column 1. Reset your margin at 53 (64) and type as for column 1.

a **Plurals ending in -oes and -os**

calicoes	altos	magnetos
cargoes	archipelagos	manifestos
dominoes	arpeggios	mementos
embargoes	cameos	memos
heroes	commandos	oratorios
innuendoes	concertos	photos
mosquitoes	crescendos	pianos
mottoes	curios	piccolos
throes	dynamos	provisos
tomatoes	embryos	ratios
tornadoes	fiascos	scherzos
torpedoes	folios	solos
volcanoes	impresarios	sopranos

b **Hyphenated words**

all-embracing	half-hour	ready-to-wear
by-product	happy-go-lucky	red-tape
chairman-elect	home-made	round-the-clock
change-over	law-abiding	second-hand
co-worker	micro-organism	self-conscious
cul-de-sac	mid-afternoon	self-employed
day-dream	mother-in-law	semi-detached
day-to-day	off-chance	seventy-seven
door-to-door	out-of-date	up-to-date
get-together	part-time	vice-chairman
good-humoured	photo-finish	work-study

Back Spacer (also tabulator key/bar) Drill 6

Set the margin at 10 (15) and tabulator at 22 (30). Type the first letter, back space and retype it, then complete the word. Tab. to the second column and repeat.
When the *first two* columns have been completed, reset the margin at 45 (56) tabulator 61 (75) and repeat as for columns one and two.

a **Wedding anniversaries**

First	Cotton	Fifteenth	Crystal
Second	Paper	Twentieth	China
Third	Leather	Twenty-fifth	Silver
Fifth	Wooden	Thirtieth	Pearl
Seventh	Woollen	Fortieth	Ruby
Tenth	Tin	Fiftieth	Golden
Twelfth	Silk and fine linen	Sixtieth	Diamond

See also Drill 8 One hundred difficult words, page 6. Drill 6 *b* Tricky spellings, page 5. Retype as in the style above.

Task 106 (b)

b)

PAVING

Item	Description	Quantity	Unit	Metric	£	p
	Excavation and Earthwork					
a (100 mm)	Excavate over site to reduce levels, average 4" deep.	227	sq. yd.	189 m²		
b (125 mm)	Ditto, average 5" deep.	69	sq. yd.	58 m²		
c (180 mm)	Ditto, average 7" deep.	20	sq. yd.	17 m²		
d (200 mm)	Ditto, average 8" deep.	190	sq. yd.	159 m²		
e	Load surplus excavated material and cart away from site.	81	cub. yd.	21 m³		
f	Grade and roll formation to falls.	32	sq. yd.	27 m²		
g	Ditto to falls and cross falls.	883	sq. yd.	738 m²		
h	Bed of ashes, as described, 4" thick, well rolled and consolidated, to falls and blinded for concrete.	32	sq. yd.			
i	Hardcore filling, as described, under pavings.	26	cub. yd.	7 m³		
j	Grade surface of hardcore to falls and cross falls and blind for concrete.	77	sq. yd.	64 m²		
k	Bed of hardcore, as described, 4" thick to falls and cross falls and blinded for concrete.	485	sq. yd.	405 m²		
l	Ditto, average 7" thick, ditto.	117	sq. yd.	99		
m	Ditto, average 8" thick, ditto.	205	sq. yd.	171		
	Concrete Work					
n	Allow here, or in the following rates, for holes, sinkings, working around pipes, gullies and the like and for making good.					
	Concrete, Quality "B", as described					
o (29 m²)	In paving, 4" thick, to falls and cross falls not exceeding 15° from horizontal, with tamped finish, laid in bays (average 35 square yards), including all formwork.	883	sq. yd.			
p (9.5 mm)	3/8" Thick "Flexcell" non-extruding impregnated cane fibre expansion joint, 4" high and sealing joint with "Pliastic" sealing compound.	333	lin. yd.	304 m		
	Carried to Collection				£	

Typist – Please make me a copy of this section of the Bill of Quantities.

- 10 -

b **Tricky spellings**

donor	desiccated	annihilate	gaseous
hygiene	destructible	oscillate	draughty
genuine	believable	manoeuvre	synonym
gaiety	alignment	tendency	glossary
epidemic	eligibility	innocence	liaison
heinous	paralleled	contretemps	discreet
desolate	exhilarate	vacillate	licensee
rhubarb	herbaceous	catechise	implicit
harass	vociferous	hysterics	funereal

See also: Drill 8 One hundred difficult words, page 6, and type as above.

Tabulator Key (also shift key) Drill 7

a Set margin at 7 (13) and tabs at 33 (40) and 55 (65) and type across the page.

Comparative ranks in HM fighting forces

Royal Navy	*Army and Royal Marines*	*Royal Air Force*
Admiral of the Fleet	Field-Marshal	Marshal of the RAF
Admiral	General	Air Chief Marshal
Vice-Admiral	Lieutenant-General	Air Marshal
Rear-Admiral	Major-General	Air Vice-Marshal
Commodore	Brigadier	Air Commodore
Captain	Colonel	Group Captain
Commander	Lieutenant-Colonel	Wing Commander
Lieutenant-Commander	Major	Squadron Leader
Lieutenant	Captain	Flight Lieutenant
Sub-Lieutenant	Lieutenant	Flying Officer
	Second Lieutenant	Pilot Officer

b Set margin at 12 (22) and tabulator stops at 28 (37), 44 (53) and 60 (68).

The thirty-six commonest words

Below is a list of the 36 commonest words, compiled by Godfrey Dewey.

In order of frequency of occurrence in 100,000 words

7310 the	1155 I	617 have	478 they
3998 of	1035 for	600 by	466 all
3280 and	846 be	589 not	458 or
2924 to	839 was	585 at	454 which
2120 a	782 as	572 this	445 will
2116 in	775 you	542 are	433 from
1345 that	727 with	529 we	411 had
1216 it	680 he	517 his	390 has
1213 is	643 on	504 but	368 one

See also: Drill 5 *a* Words ending -oes and -os page 4
Drill 5 *b* Hyphenated words page 4
Drill 6 *b* Tricky spellings page 5
Drill 8 One hundred difficult words page 6

Type as above setting tabulator stops as required in individual drills.

Task 106 (a)

Typist — Two "odd" jobs
a) Specification – General Section
b) Bill of Quantities (P.10) – change to metric measurements

a) SPECIFICATION of work required for the erection of 20 flats at Parklands, Chestnut Ave. Guildford Surrey for Mr. S. Strong.

Block at LH margin

Vernon Bridgeland FRIBA FRICS
Architect & Surveyor Highcliff Grange
Guildford

(Take in A)

GENERAL

FORM OF CONTRACT — The ~~Form of Contract~~ will be that issued under the sanction of the Royal ~~Institute~~ of British Architects (current issue).

PLANS — A copy of the approved plans shall be available on the site at all times for the use of the Architect & the Borough ~~Surveyor~~ Engineer or his representative.

INSURANCE — The Contractor shall take out an insurance for all workmen, under the Workmen's Compensation Acts, etc. the Policy to be shown to the Architect before work is started.

MATERIALS & WORKMANSHIP — All the works mentioned in this specification are to be carried out with the best materials, plant & workmanship of their respective kinds, to the entire satisfaction of the Architect.

TEMPORARY BUILDINGS — The Contractor shall provide all temporary buildings & sheds for the storage of materials & workshops, also temporary buildings for the Messroom of the workmen as required by the current Factory act. The temp. (u.c.) buildings are to be placed in suitable positions as agreed with the Architect.

OFFICE ACCOM. — The Contractor shall provide & maintain suitable temp. office accom. on the site including the provision of a telephone, for his own use.

INSPECTION OF WORK — The Contractor shall provide the necessary facilities for the inspection & measurement of the works at all times during the continuance of the works.

ORDER OF WORK — The whole of the work shall be executed in such order & sequence as agreed with the Architect. Progress Charts prepared by the Contractor & agreed by the Architect shall be adhered to.

(Change order here)

(A) The Articles of Agreement & Conditions of the Contract will be the 1980 Private Edition With Quantities issued by the Joint Contracts Tribunal under sanctions of the Royal Institute of British Architects. [SANCTIONS]

Margin Release (also shift key and tabulator key/bar)   Drill 8

Set margin at 8 (12), tabulator at 24 (32) and right-hand margin at 30 (36).
Type columns one and two, using the tabulator, and margin release, where necessary.
When completed, reset margin at 44 (51), tabulator at 61 (70) and right-hand margin at 67 (83) and type columns three and four.

One hundred difficult words

Abeyance	Confectionery	Fahrenheit	Metamorphosis
Abhorrence	Connoisseur	Fuchsia	Miscellaneous
Accelerator	Conscientious	Fulfilling	Mischievous
Accommodation	Conversable	Gramophone	Miniature
Accompanist	Convertible	Haemorrhage	Nonchalant
Acetylene	Correspondence	Handsomely	Noticeable
Adaptability	Corroborate	Humorous	Numismatic
Administrator	Cumulative	Idiosyncrasy	Obeisance
Adolescence	Customarily	Immigrate	Occasional
Aluminium	Debatable	Imperceptible	Occurrence
Antiseptic	Defamatory	Incandescent	Opportunity
Asphyxiate	Definitely	Incoherency	Oscillate
Audibility	Denouement	Inconceivable	Paraphernalia
Auxiliary	Descendant	Incontestable	Perspicacious
Benefited	Diagrammatic	Indissoluble	Posthumous
Blamable	Diaphragm	Innocuous	Privilege
Bulletin	Disagreeable	Innoxious	Pseudonym
Calligraphy	Dissentient	Intercede	Recommend
Canvasser	Divergent	Intestacy	Resuscitate
Carburettor	Ecstasy	*Jewelry	Riveted
Cemetery	Effervesce	Lavender	Separate
Chequered	Eligible	Liaison	Superintendent
Chiropodist	Embarrassment	Joquacious	Supersede
Compliance	Emissary	Mantelpiece	Tranquillize
Comprehensible	Encyclopaedia	Meanness	Unparalleled

*Jewellery/Jewelry
One example of *two* accepted spellings of the same word.

Figures (used in sentences) . Drill 9

1 Quarter Days in England are as follows: Lady Day 25 March, Midsummer 24 June, Michaelmas 29 September, and Christmas 25 December.
2 Commonwealth Day is 24 May.
3 The earliest photograph was taken by a Frenchman in 1826.
4 The oldest record in the BBC Gramophone Library was made in 1884.
5 The first men to row the Atlantic were two Norwegians in 1896.
6 The Nobel Prize was awarded for the first time on 10 December 1901.
7 The Wright brothers made the first successful flight on 17 December 1903.
8 Captain Scott reached the South Pole in 1912.
9 The RAF was formed in 1918.
10 The first experimental broadcast in England was made in December 1919.
11 Charles Lindbergh completed the first solo Atlantic flight in 1927.
12 The World's first public television broadcasting service was opened from Alexandra Palace on 2 November 1936.
13 The Second World War began 3 September 1939 and ended 15 August 1945.
14 The Coronation of Queen Elizabeth II took place on 2 June 1953.
15 The first successful manned space flight was made by Yuri Gagarin on 12 April 1961.
16 President Kennedy was assassinated on 22 November 1963.
17 The investiture of the Prince of Wales took place at Caernarvon Castle on 1 July 1969.
18 The first men to walk on the moon were Neil Armstrong and Edwin Aldrin on 20 July 1969.

2.00 EXCAVATOR

2.01 Demolition. Take down dwarf garden wall & set aside old bricks for clients use.
uc| //

2.02 Grub up concrete & brick paving & similarly set aside sound whole material. Grub up dwarf wall foundations & steps (2) or of concrete (1)
trs.

2.03 Excavate for foundations. Excavate trenches f. footings to widths & depths indicated on the drawings, return, fill & ram (trenches) selected excavated material around footings.
of

lc| 2.04. EXCAVATE FOR DRAINS. Excavate f. drains, manholes, etc as shown, up to existing manhole of new branches to existing soil & rainwater drains all to required levels & falls, grade & consolidate bottoms & return, fill in & consolidate on completion.
of

2.05 Excavate for services. Excavate f. gas, electricity & water mains allowing 10 m run of trench for ea. service at a minimum depth of 300 mm water to be in ground floor w.c. uc| stopcock|
Gas & electric meters in lobby cupboard. Return, fill in & ram trenches on completion.

2.06. Hardcore. Make up to required levels under surface concrete w. brick hardcore broken to pass around gauge, levelled, consolidated, blinded with ash or clinker to receive site concrete.

2.07. Make up to required levels under pavings with clinker.

2.08. Cart away. Cart away from site all surplus excavated material & topsoil as it accumulates.

~~2.09~~ 2.03 Strip Site. Excavate over the whole area of the works & pavings to the depths & levels shown on the drawings. Wheel & cart away from site to tips.
lc|

Please change numbers accordingly.

on drawing No. W.D. 1/5776

Substitute for 1.02 on p.1 //
The Contract shall be a "FIRM PRICE" Contract & the Form of Contract Agreement & Schedule of Conditions shall be the J.C.T. Standard Form of Building Contract, Private Edition With Quantities, 1963 Edition (July 1977 Revision) incorporating Amendment No 15/1978

Underscoring (underlining) Drill 10

Having typed each group of words to be underscored, return the carriage so that the printing point is directly under the first letter, then, with the shift lock down, strike the underscore key for as many spaces as there are letters and spaces. Final punctuation is better not underscored.

Sources of Information

There are many occasions in an office when a secretary needs information which she cannot supply from her own knowledge. It is then that she should know exactly where to look for it, and which book to consult. The following will help her:

1 Names and initials, addresses and telephone numbers can be verified in the Telephone Directory, or the Electoral Roll (obtainable from the Town Hall). Yellow Pages, a classified directory of businesses and telephone numbers, provides useful information.

2 Many offices now use teleprinters which can be linked up to a special Telex telephone circuit. There are separate Telex Directories available for this purpose, giving the relevant information.

3 The Post Office publishes useful books: Postal Addresses and Index to Postcode Directories, which lists all towns and villages with their counties and postcodes, and the Post Office Guide, which gives full details of postal services, together with other facilities such as the Giro Bank, National Savings, motor vehicle and other types of licence, and information on obtaining passports.

4 In addition to the above, and as a result of the mechanised process used by the Post Office to speed delivery of mail, Postcode Directories are published – one for each city and major town, with the surrounding districts which are included in the same Postcode area. These Directories can be consulted at all main Post Offices.

5 The main books giving information on travel are the Automobile Association Members' Handbook, the Royal Automobile Club Guide and Handbook, the ABC Railway Guide, the ABC World Airways Guide and the ABC Shipping Guide.

6 The forms of address, together with decorations, honours, etc. can be found in Black's Titles and Forms of Address, while in addition, information on individuals who have distinguished themselves in some way is available in Debrett's Peerage and Baronetage, Who's Who (Who Was Who, etc.).

7 For general information of a varied kind, Whitaker's Almanack and Pears Cyclopaedia are indispensable.

8 Hansard is the verbatim record of proceedings in Parliament. This and all Government Reports are published by Her Majesty's Stationery Office.

9 There are many year books giving general information and others giving details of people in various professions, as Crockford's Clerical Directory, Directory of Directors, etc.

10 No office should be without a good Dictionary, Roget's Thesaurus of English Words and Phrases, Fowler's Modern English Usage, and a good typewriting reference book.

Practice Tasks – Figures and Special Characters

Task 1 Scientific Work

In the typing of fractions (not using the solidus) all figures should be on the same level, i.e. providing there are no inferior characters, the line separating the numerator from the denominator will be typed immediately under the numerator (as if underscored). To type the denominator, the figures should be one space below, providing there are no superior characters. Should there be any superior or inferior characters, an extra half space should be left for the whole expression.

If a number of superior or inferior characters appear in any one line, it is quicker to leave the necessary spaces, and, when the line is completed, to go back to the first space, raise or lower the carriage half a space as required, and then continue along the line, typing in the characters.

Whole numbers, or signs for multiplication or division of the whole expression should be centred vertically between the fractions.

Fractions must be centrally placed over or under the line separating the numerator from the denominator.

The examples given should be carefully studied and practiced:

1 $\text{Volume of } 0_2 \text{ in room} = \dfrac{10 \times 20 \times 20 \times 21}{100} = 840 \text{ m}^3$

2 $V_1 = \dfrac{P_2 V_2}{P_1} = \dfrac{450 \times 3}{600} = 2.25 \text{ m}^3$

3 $P = \dfrac{720 \text{ kN}}{\text{m}^2} \times 0.45 \text{ m} \times 2.25 \text{ m}^2 \times \dfrac{400 \text{ Hz}}{60} \times \dfrac{1}{1000}$

Task 105

SPECIFICATION of works to be carried out and materials to be used in the erection and completion of Offices at Fleetlands, Seaford, Sussex under the supervision of and to the complete satisfaction of:-

Wiseman & Williams

Chartered Architects
Surveyors
Heather Gardens
Seaford, Sussex

May 19--

1.00 GENERAL CONDITIONS

1.01 ~~Contract Form~~ Form of Contract. The Contractor will be required to enter into a Contract for due and proper execution of the works.

1.02 The Agreement and Schedule of Conditions of Building Contract, will be the form issued under the sanction of the R.I.B.A. dated 1963 Private Edition (Without Quantities) Revised.

See next page

1.03 Where the Clauses in this Specification are at variance with the Form of Contract, then the Clauses in this Specification shall be binding.

1.04 The following Clauses will be deleted completely from the Form of Contract:-

Article 4A
Clause 10 (Clerk of Works)
Clause 20B and C
Clause 31 (Fluctuations)

1.05 The Contractor shall read in conjunction with every portion of this Specification the Agreement, and the work, together with the aforesaid agreement, shall be executed in strict accordance with this Specification and the drawing numbered W.D.1/~~5776.~~ 3221

1.06 The following will be inserted in the Appendix to the Agreement:-

Clauses 15, 16 and 30:	Defects Liability Period	6 months
Clause 21:	Date for Possession	A date 7 days subsequent to date of Agreement.
	Date for Completion	The period to be agreed
~~Clause 22:~~	~~Liquidated & Ascertained Damages~~	~~£25 per month~~
Clause 30(1):	Period for interim certificates	Monthly
	Period for honouring certificates	14 days
Clause 30(3):	Percentage to be retained	10 per cent
	Limit of retention fund	5 per cent
Clause 30(5):	Period of final measurement	6 months

(continued)

Task 2 Mechanical Equivalent of Heat

The great task of measuring the quantity of heat-energy which is equal to a certain amount of work (§ §25, 49), and so of comparing the invisible motion of molecules with the visible motion of masses, was attempted and triumphantly accomplished by Joule in 1843 when the modern theory of energy was founded. One heat-unit is equal to 777 foot-pounds. In other words, if a mass of 1 lb. were to be pulled down by gravity through 777 feet, and the whole of its kinetic energy changed into heat in 1 lb. of water at 32°, the temperature of the water would be thereby raised to 33°. Thus we can measure the work done by heat in melting 1 lb. of ice at 32° (§ 69) and find it to be equal to 112,000 foot-pounds, while that done in evaporating 1 lb. of water at 212° (§ 70) is 751,000 foot-pounds. It appears that the heating of $1\frac{1}{2}$ lb of ice at 32° until it becomes steam at 212° requires as much energy as the feat of mountain-climbing described in § § 49, 52.

Task 3 Fractions and Dead Keys

A typist whose work involves the frequent use of accents can have keys for accents fitted on her machine in place of keys that she seldom uses. Typists use the fractions $\frac{1}{4}$, $\frac{1}{2}$, $\frac{3}{4}$, but less frequently use the keys for $\frac{1}{8}$, $\frac{3}{8}$, $\frac{5}{8}$, $\frac{7}{8}$ – and they can always be represented by typing ordinary figures separated by the solidus, eg 1/8, 3/8, 5/8, 7/8.

When using 'dead keys', the accent should always be typed first (as the carriage does not move forward) followed by the letter over which it is to appear. A typewriter mechanic can change one key for another quite quickly. It is also possible to have detachable accent keys, which are pressed on when required. When using them, however, it is necessary to backspace each time as they are not 'dead keys', and therefore move on a space when depressed.

Electronic typewriters must be fitted with an international selector switch in order to use an international daisy wheel which includes accents.

Typists whose work involves correspondence with the dollar countries can have keys for the dollar and cent symbols included on the keyboard or daisy wheel.

Task 4 The Old £sd

The old pounds, shillings and pence (£sd) have long been forgotten since decimalization of our currency in February 1971. However, it is still necessary to know that the shillings and pence, being abbreviations, were always followed by a full stop, i.e., s. d. but not the £, which was – as it is today – a sign.

Typists should know how to type amounts using £sd as they may have to refer back to documents or invoices and quote from them. They should know that 50p was typed as 10s. or 10/–, that £1.83 was £1 16s. 7d. and that on invoices the @ sign was usually followed by the solidus (/), eg 3 reams @ 15/– ream.

4 Whole numbers or signs for multiplication, division, etc. of the whole expression should be centred vertically between the fractions.

5 Any signs or symbols not on the typewriter should be added afterwards by hand, in an ink as close to the colour of the ribbon as possible.

Task 104

Typist Please let me have 2 copies (1+1) of the following. L & R margins ½". Leave 3 or 4 spaces between each group of figures – & pay special attention to alignment.

NOTES FOR LECTURE 2B

Source

1. $T_n = \frac{a(4-r^n)}{1-r}$ FSP/79

2. $T = c\left[\frac{(2+b)^n - 2}{b}\right]$ BC/49

3. $Y \frac{b_2}{3-x} + \frac{a_3}{(2+x)^2} + \frac{b_n}{(2+x)^n}$ FSP/94

4. $5\,\frac{a^2+b^3-c^2}{2abc} + 4\,\frac{b^2+c^3}{4ab}$ QA/80

6 5. $7\,\frac{(ab)^3-(bc)^2}{3(abc)^3} - 2\,\frac{(a+b)^3-(2a-b)^2}{4(bc)^2}$ QA/102

6. $V_1 = \frac{P_2 V_2}{P_1} = \frac{450 \times 3}{600} = 2.25\ ft^3$ SSS/63

7. $V = \frac{n}{n-1}\, m R T_1 \left[\left(\frac{P_2}{P_1}\right)^{(n-1)} - 1\right]$ GA/207

8. $I = \frac{3500 \times 175}{0.8}$ ft-lb EB/54

9. $E = \frac{329150}{4.2 \times 12^3}$ kWh EB/78

10. $t = \sqrt{\frac{\Sigma f(y-3)^2}{n}}$ RA/300

5 11. $7\,\frac{a^3+b^3+c^3}{4a+2b+c} + 3\,\frac{a^2-c^2}{a+2b-c}$ QA/81

2 International Standards Organization (ISO)

This country has for many years now adopted international paper sizes, the 24-hour clock and metric measurements to fall in line with international standards. These are explained below.

International paper sizes

The ISO system is based on the principle of proportional relationship of one size of paper to another. Thus, any sheet of paper (identified by the letter A and a number) folded in half provides the next size down. The A series of paper goes from A0, 841 x 1189 mm, to A7, 74 x 105 mm, the two most common sizes being A4 210 x 297 mm, and A5, 148 x 210 mm.

A4 can be divided as shown below:

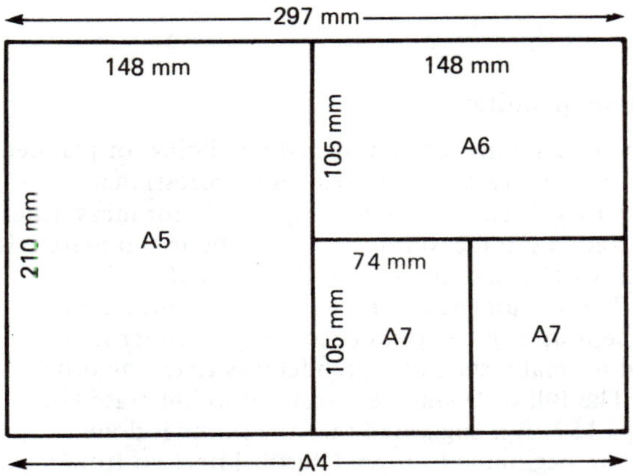

Uses of paper

A4 Letters
Literary work
Specifications
Reports, etc

A5 Letters
Memoranda (used 'portrait' or 'landscape')

A6 Postcards

A7 Compliments slips
Business cards

The ISO paper sizes are based on metric measurements so the measurements in inches are approximate only.

The table on page 10 shows the comparative sizes of paper and is for general information only, as it is assumed that the student will already be completely familiar with the International sizes of paper and will be able to set margins automatically, according to the type and length of work and with the use of the scales on the typewriter.

Time – The twenty-four hour clock

The 24-hour clock which is in use for all air and rail traffic movement is universally used in the Services and as the normal method of telling the time on the Continent.

1 The 24-hour time system begins at 0001 (ie one minute after midnight) and ends at 2359 (ie one minute before midnight) to avoid date ambiguity.

2 There must always be four unpunctuated figures in the time. These should be followed by the word hours (written out or abbreviated, with or without full stops according to style of punctuation used), eg 1030 hrs, 1510 hrs.

3 Any time up to 1159 hrs indicates the morning period, eg 0520 hrs, 0845 hrs, 1018 hrs.

The afternoon, evening and night periods begin at 1200 hrs. and continue until 2359 hrs., eg 1205 hrs, 1840 hrs, 2250 hrs.

4 In speech say 'twelve hundred hours', 'twelve-o-five hours', 'eighteen forty hours' and 'twenty-two fifty hours'.

The heading. An explanatory paragraph:

a Hanging paragraph at 3 in. with $\frac{1}{2}$ in. indent.
b The word 'Specification' is typed in spaced capitals (with two spaces after it), or in closed capitals.
c In double spacing, but the name and address of the architect is in single spacing, each line indented $\frac{1}{2}$ in. ending in line with the right-hand margin.
d Date, beginning at left-hand margin or ending at right-hand margin, three spaces from both the heading and the body.

Side headings (within margin)

a Begin at one inch.
b Typed in closed capitals and usually underscored.
c Always in single spacing.

Body of work

a Margin at $2\frac{1}{2}$ in. with indent of $\frac{1}{2}$ in.
b 'Trades' (bricklayer, carpenter, etc.) heading centred over the line of type, usually about an inch down from last section, or on a fresh page.

Tabular stops. These should be set at one inch, 3 in. and $3\frac{1}{2}$ in. with left-hand marginal stop at $2\frac{1}{2}$ in.

Engineers' specifications – traditional

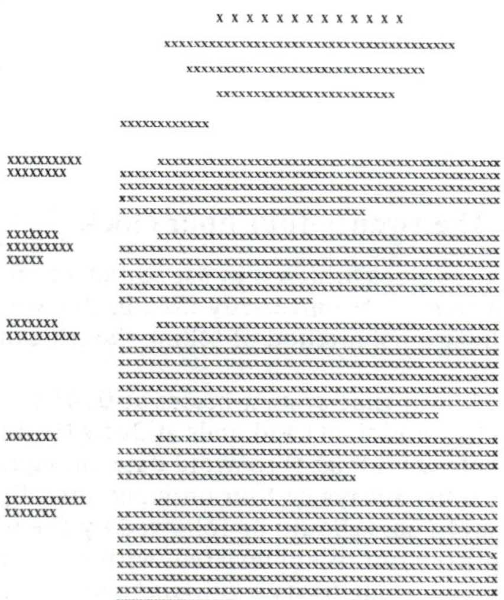

These are similar to the traditional builders' specification, except that the main heading is centred and displayed over the body of the work.

Engineers' specifications – blocked

These are similar to the builders' blocked specification except that the main heading is often blocked to the left-hand margin.

Engineers' specifications – semi-blocked

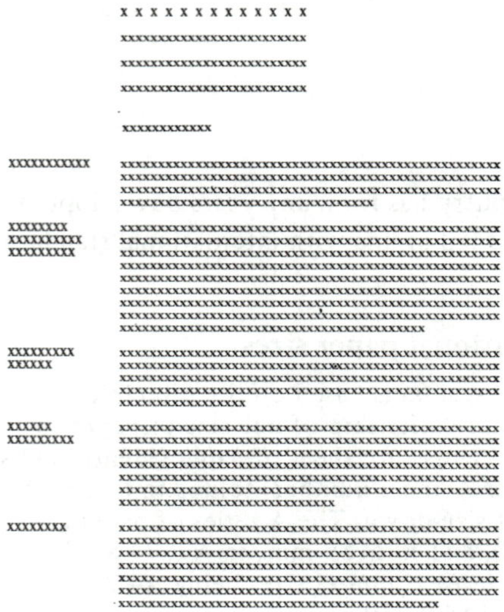

These are similar to the blocked style, except that there are side headings within the margin, as in the traditional style.

Bill of quantities

When an architect has designed a building, or planned a reconstruction, he approaches a professional Quantity Surveyor, who is responsible for measuring it, trade by trade, on the basis of labour and materials, etc. which are necessary for the particular job.

This document is then sent out to builders who price it up and the total becomes the tender figure, and normally the lowest tenderer is given the order.

The Bill of Quantities is set out as illustrated on page 157. It is suggested that the ruling is done before beginning to type. (Vertical lines go from edge to edge of the page.)

Mathematical and scientific formulae

1 In mathematical and scientific expressions figures should be on the same level; the line separating the numerator from the denominator should be typed immediately under the numerator (as if underscored), and the denominator figures should be one space below.
2 An extra half space should be allowed for the whole line where there are superior and inferior characters.
3 Figures should be centrally placed in both the numerator and the denominator.

Comparative sizes of paper

Nearest equivalents of International and Imperial Sizes

	International		Imperial	
	Measurements			*Measurements in inches*
No	*mm*	*inches*	*Name*	
A0	841 x 1189	$33\frac{1}{8}''$ x $46\frac{3}{4}''$	Double Elephant	$26\frac{3}{4}''$ x $40''$
A1	594 x 841	$23\frac{3}{8}''$ x $33\frac{1}{8}''$	Imperial	$22''$ x $30''$
A2	420 x 594	$16\frac{1}{2}''$ x $23\frac{3}{8}''$	Half Imperial	$15''$ x $22''$
A3	297 x 420	$11\frac{3}{4}''$ x $16\frac{1}{2}''$	(Brief	$13''$ x $16''$
			(Draft	$10''$ x $16''$
			(Foolscap	$8''$ x $13''$
A4	210 x 297	$8\frac{1}{4}''$ x $11\frac{3}{4}''$	(Quarto (post)	$7''$ x $9''$
			(Quarto	$8''$ x $10''$
A5	148 x 210	$5\frac{7}{8}''$ x $8\frac{1}{4}''$	(Sixmo	$6\frac{1}{2}''$ x $8''$
			(Octavo	$5''$ x $8''$
A6	105 x 148	$4\frac{1}{8}''$ x $5\frac{7}{8}''$	–	–
A7	74 x 105	$2\frac{7}{8}''$ x $4\frac{1}{8}''$	–	–

Number of spaces and average number of words in typescript

	A4 portrait	A5 portrait
Spaces across the page		
Elite (12 to the inch)	99	70
Pica (10 to the inch)	82	58
Lines down the page		
Elite and Pica (6 to the inch)	70	50
Average number of words on page		
$1''$ Margins all round		
Elite	870	342
Pica	696	289
$1\frac{1}{2}''$ Left; $1''$ right, top and bottom		
Elite	812	–
Pica	638	–

14 Technical

Specifications

A specification is a document which sets out the work to be undertaken by a contractor *on any given project*, giving the details, by trade, of how the work is to be carried out, and what materials are to be used.

In the building trade, specifications are usually written by an architect, though a builder might make out his own if the particular job were very small.

There is no *one* correct display for the typing of specifications as each firm has its own preference. There are, however, certain guiding principles which are adopted for each of the styles used by builders and engineers.

Spacing can be single or double according to preference. Double line spacing is easier for the men on the site to read, but if the specification is very long, single is more economical and less bulky when put into book form.

Diagrammatical displays are given below:

Builders' Specifications—Blocked

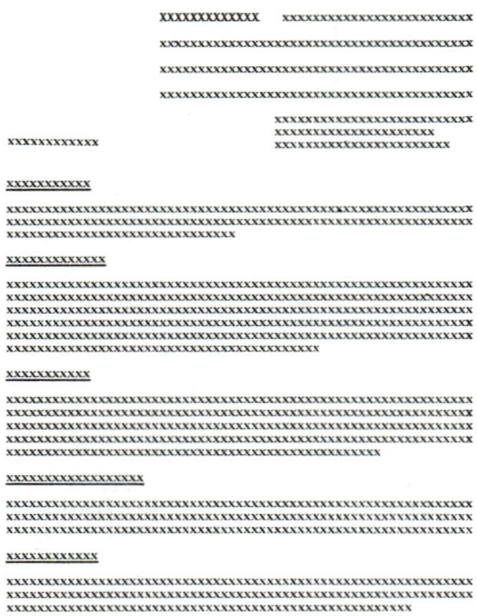

Heading

a Block paragraph: begin at $3\frac{1}{2}$ in., right-hand margin $\frac{1}{2}$ to $\frac{3}{4}$in. main margin.
b The word 'Specification' in closed capitals.
c Double spacing. Name of architect, blocked, in single line spacing beginning at 5 in. and ending $\frac{1}{2}$ in. from right-hand margin or block at margin.

Body of work

a Blocked paragraphs.
b Margin of one to two inches to allow for numbers (*see* '*e*') and stitching margin.
c 'Trades' heading up to margin—each trade beginning a new page.
d Side headings up to margin and underscored. Paragraphs to continue on same line or blocked two spaces down.
e Some architects number each trade, and paragraph within the trade; these will be typed within the margin (*see* page 154).

Builders' Specifications—Traditional

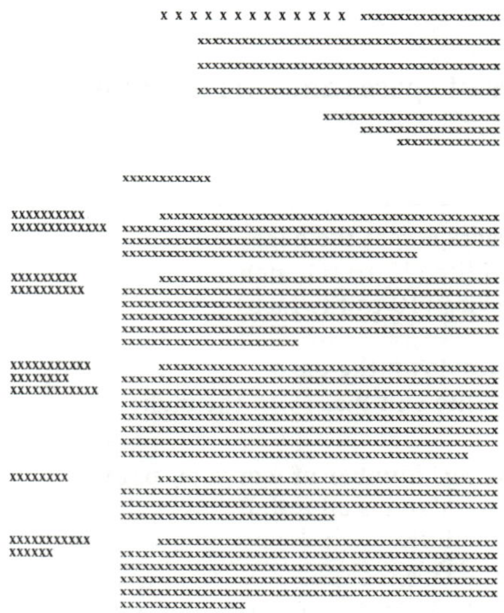

These are divided into three parts: the heading, the side headings and the body of the work.

International envelope sizes

ISO envelopes are designed to accommodate A sizes of paper, either folded or flat. Envelopes are known by the letters B and C followed by the number corresponding to the A size of paper. The size DL, however, really belongs to the C series.

The B series is designed to take the larger sizes of paper, documents, etc., and also to accommodate without folding a C series envelope if a stamped, addressed envelope or business reply envelope is to be enclosed. This series, however, and some of the C series is not yet fully established in this country.

The envelopes most used are the C6, 114 mm x 162 mm ($4\frac{1}{2}''$ x $6\frac{3}{8}''$), and the DL, 110 mm x 220 mm ($4\frac{1}{4}''$ x $8\frac{5}{8}''$).

The C6 envelope takes A5 paper folded in half, and A4 folded in half twice.

The DL envelope takes A4 folded equally into three.

Typing of money

General rules for typing decimal currency:

1 **Use of full stop**

a Neither the £ symbol nor the p are followed by a full stop, except where this is used after either at the end of a sentence.

b The decimal point is typed on the base line, as for a full stop, but in written or printed matter it will appear raised to the centre of the figures.

2 **Amounts in pounds only**

Amounts in exact pounds will follow the pound symbol £1, £5, £10, £100, £1,000.

Note: If the decimal point should be used, as in accounting, it must be followed by two noughts: £1·00, £5·00.

3 **Mixed amounts of pounds and pence**

Any sum over £1 should be shown as a decimal: £1.20, £7.50, £10.75. The use of pence alone for amounts greater than £1 is incorrect.

4 **Amounts in pence only**

a Amounts in pence only can be typed with or without the decimal point. (*Note*: The £ symbol and p abbreviation never appear together in the same expression.)

20p	25p	50p	75p	90p
£0.20	£0.25	£0.50	£0.75	£0.90

b Following the decimal point there should always be two digits to avoid possible confusion: £0.50, £0.05.

c The halfpenny, no longer legal tender, was shown as a fraction in the normal way:

£0.88½ £0.04½ £0.00½

5 **Expression of amounts in column form**

a The £ symbol should head the column both for amounts in exact pounds, or for amounts in pounds and pence:

£	£	£
170.50	100	56.50
25.65	2,000	3.70
250.00	30	90.00
.30	56,220	7.05
£446.45	£58,350	£157.25

The £ sign may appear over the unit column of the pounds, when pence are also used in the same expression. However, many typists are placing it over the decimal point to achieve a more balanced display. It should be centred over the longest line if pounds only are used unless blocked at the left-hand margin.

b Amounts on invoices can be typed in two ways:

i If one column appears on the printed invoice, amounts will be typed as above in 5*a*.

ii If two columns appear on the printed invoice, the pounds will appear in the first column, and pence in the second.

£	p
1	30
4	25
7	05
	75
10	00
£23	35

6 **The typing of cheques**

Banks do not recommend that cheques be typed, but in large business concerns where this may be economically desirable, the following rule is laid down (March 1984): 'No indemnity is required where the words and figures are entered on cheques by mechanical means and a fully inked, acid-proof ribbon is used in the machine or a satisfactory incision is made on the paper by the machine.' Figures should be typed as a decimal at all times, eg. £84.00, £10.50, £3.05, £0.75 and may be expressed in figures, unless there are no pounds, eg Eighty-four pounds only. Ten pounds 50. Three pounds 05. *but* Seventy-five pence.

Task 103

Typist Will you please type a copy of the Menu & Toast List for the Town Gardeners Association.

Front page

The Town Gardeners' Assoc. – (Caps)
POOLE BRANCH

FIFTH ANNUAL DINNER

THE BRADLEY HOTEL,
BOURNEMOUTH

Sat 9th Feb. 19..

Inside 1

MENU

Paté Maison

Cream of Asparagus

Sole Marguerite

Roast Aylesbury Duckling
Orange Sauce
New potatoes
Garden Peas

Peach Melba

Coffee

Inside 2

TOAST LIST

"THE QUEEN"

To propose The President
Mr. Walter Seabrooke, MBE FRHS

"THE TOWN GARDENERS ASSOC."

To propose Sir Percy Chobham MP

To reply The Chairman
Mr. Eric Rose MC, FRHS

"THE GUESTS"

To propose Mrs E. Calvert
To reply Mr. Basil Binks

Typist
Display so as to keep each of the 3 toasts separate.

Metrication – Système International (SI)

Students will probably be familiar with the names of some of the units, symbols and prefixes of the international metric system, generally known as SI, but they should know how to represent them in typescript. It is suggested that they study the rules and copy the examples given below.

1 There are certain base units of the SI system, from which other units are derived, the most common being the 'metre' for length, 'kilogram' (or kilogramme) for weight, 'litre' for volume of liquids, and 'degree Celsius' (formerly termed 'degree Centigrade') for temperature.

2 Each unit is represented by a symbol, a space being left before it, eg

1 m = 1 metre 1 kg = 1 kilogram 26°C 1 ℓ = 1 litre

Note: Litre is always *written* ℓ (with a loop) to avoid confusion with one (1). Metric symbols are *never* followed by a full stop.

3 A symbol never takes an 's' in the plural, except when the unit is written out.

5 m = 5 metres 12 kg = 12 kilograms 4 ℓ = 4 litres
2 t = 2 tonnes

4 All units are typed in lower-case letters, except when they are named after a scientist, or when a capital letter is used for the symbol, eg

J = joule kJ = kilojoule MJ = megajoule A = ampere
V = volt W = watt

5 Prefixes are used to indicate the quantity by which a unit is multiplied,

kilo = 1000: kilometre = 1000 metres; kilogram = 1000 grams

milli indicates a thousandth of a unit, eg millimetre, milligram. Most prefixes are typed with a small letter, but capitals are used for tera = T, giga = G, mega = M. *All* prefixes, however, take a small letter when written out in full, and are *never* followed by a hyphen.

6 A space is left between the symbols of separate (derived) units, but not after a prefix, eg

kW = kilowatt, but kW h = kilowatt hour; kV but kV h

7 If two units are multiplied together, a space must be left between the symbols, eg

m s = metres times seconds, but note: ms = milliseconds

8 The oblique (solidus) sign '/' is used to represent 'per', with no space before or after it, eg

35.5 kg/m^3 = 35.5 kilograms per cubic metre;
60 km/h = 60 km per hour

9 Symbols for 'square' and 'cube' are a *small* figure 2 or 3 slightly raised. On the typewriter it is preferable to type 'sq m', 'cu m' unless the typescript is in $1\frac{1}{2}$ or double spacing, when superior characters can be used, eg

15 m^2 = 15 sq m; 9 m^3 = 9 cu m; m^2/kg; J/m^3; W/m^2 sr

Numbers:

a Where a number is less than one, a nought must precede a decimal point, eg

0.125 m; 0.5 k

b Long numbers should be typed in groups of three with a space between to avoid using the comma as a thousands marker, though where there are only four figures, no space is necessary. (This is done to avoid confusion, as on the Continent the comma is used to represent the decimal point.) For example:

£4 350 000 £960 410 but 2000 km

Task 102

Typist Please type the following list under column headings to show date + time (a.m. or p.m.) of arrivals for the Woodland Preservation Society Conference (11–13 May). Each area to be in alphabetical order + names also within the areas. Display so that each group is clear. Ditto marks are not necessary.

May 9		a.m.	Mr. A. Phillips	London
			Mr. and Mrs. P. Adam	"
May 10		p.m.	Mr. + Mrs. B. Jonson	South Western
			Mr. + Mrs. T. White	" "
			Mr. A. Johnson	" "
			Mr. C. Richards	Southampton
			Mr. T. Bosworth	"
			Mr. + Mrs. D. Carden	"
			Mr. + Mrs. F. Sampson	East Anglia
			Mr. + Mrs. S. Paul	"
			Mr. + Mrs. F. Peters	
			Mr. + Mrs. A. F. Johns	South Eastern
			Mr. + Mrs. P. Chadwick	
	11	am	Mr. S. A. Potter	S/ton
			Miss F. Flinch	
			Mr. ~~A.~~ B Gerrard	S/W
			Mr. + Mrs. S. Gorse	S/ton
			Mr. + Mrs. W. Fairtree	
	9	pm.	Mr. + Mrs. R. Robins	S/E
			Mr. + Mrs. T. Flowers	
			Mr. + Mrs. M. Greenfern	
	10	am	Mr. + Mrs. T. Marsh	E/A
			Mr. + Mrs. G. Forrest	
	10	pm	Mr. B. Freshwater	London
			Miss I. Gardener	"
			Mr. + Mrs. S. Fountain	
	10	am	Mr. + Mrs. T. Bushby	S/ton

'GORSE'

Note:
1. area to go before name.
2. add a narrow column at end headed: 'Room No.'
3. Head up with name of conference + date

9th Mr. + Mrs. J. Potter (London) pm.
Mr. + Mrs. F. King (")
11th Mr. + ~~Mrs.~~ S. Dewe (S/W) am.
Mr. P. Redfern (London)

3 Punctuation

It is difficult to believe that in olden times books were printed without any punctuation marks, though even today, in legal documents, punctuation is usually omitted. This means, of course, that such documents have to be worded so that the meaning is perfectly clear and there can be no possibility of misinterpretation.

The typist must have a sound knowledge of punctuation because the executive when dictating rarely indicates it. He should be able to leave this aspect of the work to his typist. In audio work, however, it is customary to include some punctuation in the dictation. On the other hand, the typist must be prepared to accept the style of the executive, who may like, or dislike, the frequent use of commas, and who may have strong views on the use of capital letters.

With sentence construction generally becoming less complex, punctuation is tending towards simplicity and is chiefly a matter of logic. The following notes using full punctuation will help the typist to understand the functions of the different punctuation marks.

The full stop (full point *or* period)

The full stop is used:

1 To denote the end of a sentence:
We thank you for your letter.

2 After the initials denoting Christian names (*note* space immediately before surname):
G. S. J. Benson, Esq. *or* G.S.J. Benson, Esq.

3 After the initials denoting degrees, etc, following a person's name (*note* one space only after comma separating groups.

Captain J. W. McPherson, D.S.O., M.A., Litt.D.

4 After general abbreviations:
P.T.O., MS., pp.
Note that certain abbreviations, particularly acronyms and those used with open punctuation do not take a stop:
per cent, IOU, UNESCO, EFTA. (*see* page 14).

5 For the decimal point (which is not raised, except in advanced technical work):

52.5, 1.03, 0.65.

6 In the typing of all decimal currency – pounds £4.20, dollars $5.25, francs 10.50 F., etc.

7 To separate hours from minutes:
7.05 a.m., 9.15 p.m.
Note: International times: 0705 hrs., 2115 hrs. which are always of four figures without stops.

8 To indicate ellipsis, ie that some word or words have been omitted. Examples are based on the sentences in which passages are omitted at the beginning, middle, and end.
a The actual words used were '. . . provided your clients agree to this course before the end of the month.'
b The actual words used were: 'We believe we can do as you request . . . before the end of the month.'
c The actual words used were: 'We believe we can do as you request provided your clients agree to this course . . .'
Note: Three spaced or unspaced dots show omissions.

9 To form 'leader dots' which are intended to help carry the eyes from one point to another. The following rules should be noted:
a Dots should be typed with a light touch.
b There should be at least *one* space before the first dot, and *one* space after the last dot, to separate them from the rest of the work.
c The dots should be typed uniformly under each other throughout the passage in any one piece of work.
d Dots should be typed in one of the following ways, according to the amount of space between the columns concerned:

i Single dots with spaces between each
. . . .

ii Two dots with 3 spaces between each group
.. ..

iii Three dots with 2 spaces between each group
... ...

iv Spaced dots . . . .

v Continuous dots ....

Task 101

Typist a) Please type this itinerary as an A6 leaflet (A5 folded) keeping to display suggested (note asterisk at foot)
b) Type an Air Timetable as an A7 leaflet. Heading for P.1 similar to the A6 leaflet, but add "Outward + Return flights (Local times)". For pp. 2, 3 + 4, extract dates, times of flights, flight nos. + Air Lines.

MANAGING DIRECTOR [VISIT TO [PARIS, BORDEAUX AND ROME
17 TO 26 JUNE 19..

page 1

17 JUNE (Monday)

0805 hrs	dep	BIRMINGHAM Flight No. BA 968 (British Airways)
1010 hrs	arr	PARIS (Charles de Gaulle) Monsieur Pierre Gautier will meet you + be yr. escort whilst in Paris Acc. booked at Hotel Georges V, Avenue Georges V (Tel: 723 54 00)* for 2 nights

19 JUNE (Wednesday)

pages 2 + 3

1030 hrs	dep	PARIS (Charles de Gaulle) Flight No. IT 441 (Air Inter)
1135 hrs	arr	BORDEAUX Monsieur Henri Chabrol will meet you + escort you whilst in Bordeaux Acc. booked at Hotel Aquitaine, Parc des Expositions (Tel. 50 83 80)* for 2 nights

21 JUNE (Fri)

1120 hrs	dep	BORDEAUX Flight No IT 677 (Air Inter) Touch down at Toulouse + Marseille
1310	arr	NICE – Lunch at airport
1525	d	NICE Flight No AZ 339 (Alitalia)
1625	a	ROME (Leonardo da Vinci) Signor Francesco Salvi will meet you + escort you whilst in Rome Acc. booked at Hotel Savoia, Via Ludovisi (48 71 41)* for 5 nights

26 JUNE (Tues)

1600 hrs	dep	ROME (L da V) Flight No AZ 290 (Alitalia)
1730	a	LONDON (Heathrow)
1930	d	" (") Flight No BD 780 (British Midlands)
2015	a	BIRMINGHAM Co. car will meet you at the airport

page 4 List the 3 hotels with their addresses + tel. nos.
* Do not give addresses + tel. of hotels on any other page.

e No letters or words should extend beyond the line of dots.

10 In the formation of combination characters as in the exclamation mark !

Note: No stop is used at the end of a heading unless it follows a recognized abbreviation.

Open punctuation means the omission of all full stops and commas in the following parts of letters: date, inside address, salutation, complimentary close, designation, enclosure.

Within the body of the letter, abbreviations are typed without stops and are closed up: eg ie am. A person's initials are typed without the stop, but with a space between. Initials of degrees, etc., following a name are typed without a space: Mr F A Fisher OBE BSc.

The colon

The colon is used:

1 To introduce a quotation (although a comma *may* be used): the speaker said: 'This is my greatest triumph.'

2 To introduce a series of items within a sentence:
We have these shoes in the following colours: blue, black, brown or beige.

3 To introduce a series of items (with or without a following hyphen) when a series of items follows as an inset passage:
The following should be included in our new requisition:

letterheads	pencils	drawing-pins
envelopes	rubbers	steel-pins
postcards	rulers	paper-clips

4 To introduce a self-contained statement:
This is my idea: to store all existing files and install a completely modern filing system.

5 To join two clauses or sentences in juxtaposition, often with contrasting meanings:
We are never deceived: we deceive ourselves.

The semicolon

The semicolon is used mainly to separate a clause or phrase from a following clause or phrase – often replacing the conjunction 'and' eg Joan neglected to practise her scales; gradually her technique deteriorated.

The comma

The comma is used:

1 To separate clauses in a sentence.

2 To separate items in a list (or a series of adjectives):
Club members can play tennis, squash, cricket and golf. (*Note*: Comma before 'and' is not necessary *but* My cousin invited the cast, the understudies, the technicians, the orchestra, and the world-famous conductor, to a cocktail party.)

Note: The comma before the 'and' emphasises the word, and suggests that 'even' is implied. On logical grounds it would be better to use a comma before 'and' in any list, but this is not customary in the printing world.

3 To mark off a descriptive passage from the main sentence (acting as parenthesis)'
Mr. John Webster, the new local representative, called to see the Manager.

4 After such words as *however*, *therefore*, *nevertheless*, at the beginning of a sentence, and before and after them when they occur within the sentence.

5 Before the abbreviations ie, eg, Esq, viz, et seq, etc, and at the end of the following clause.

Note: No comma should follow these abbreviations unless the sense requires it as in the last sentence.

6 In letters (typed in the traditional form):
a After each line of inside address, except the last.
b Following the salutation.
c After the complimentary close.

7 In figures to separate the hundreds, thousands and millions, eg 5,150,780.

Note: Commas are not used in the following cases:
a Date: 1980.
b Policy and Bond numbers: XB 79412.
c Invoice and order numbers: No. 122419.
d After the decimal point: 31.3241
e Numbers of houses: 1093 Central Parade, New York.

The apostrophe

The apostrophe is used:

1 To indicate the possessive case:
The girls' coats. The girl's coat.

2 To indicate elision:
I don't think he will come.

3 To represent the sign for foot or feet, as 20'.

4 To represent the sign for minutes in geographical measurements as 69°25' N.

5 To form combination characters, as !

6 As single quotation marks (*see* Inverted Commas).

Note: Apostrophes are no longer required in:
a Plurals of figures: the 50s, size 6s.
b Plural forms of abbreviations: MPs., MOs., unless confusion would arise: *mind your ps and qs* but *dot your i's*.

Task 100 (continued)

Thursday, 9th September

9.30 a.m.		Poet's Restaurant, Shanklin Prop. Mr + Mrs W. Clarke.
10.45 a.m.		The Old Village Hotel, Shanklin Manageress: Mrs. J. Worne
12.00 ~~p.m.~~ noon	dep.	Shanklin by taxi.
12.15 p.m.	arr.	The Blue Lagoon, Bonchurch, for lunch with Proprietor: Mr. V. Jakes.
2.30 p.m.	dep.	Bonchurch by car with Mr. May.
2.45 p.m.	arr.	The Cascade Hotel, Ventnor Manageress: Mrs. L. Bryant.
4.00 p.m.		The George Hotel, Ventnor Prop: Mr. B. Townsend
5.30 p.m.	arr.	The Undercliffe Hotel, Niton Manager: Mr. G. Tanner
7.30 p.m.	arr.	The Hurst Arms, ~~Newport~~ (Dinner at) NEWPORT (Accom. booked for one night.) Manager: Mr. A. Martin

/N

Friday, 10th September

9.30 a.m.		The Central, Newport. Manageress: Miss M. Dew.
10.40 a.m.	dep.	Newport by car with Mr. May
11.15 am	arr.	The Downs Hotel, Freshwater Props. Mr. + Mrs. S. Watson
12.45 p.m.	arr.	Lunch at The Welcome Inn, Yarmouth with Manageress: Mrs. W. Carr
3.15 p.m.	arr.	The Yachtsman, Cowes Props Mr. + Mrs. J. Petts
4.30 p.m.		The Standard Hotel, Cowes Manager: Mr. F. Lake
7.30 p.m.	dep.	Ryde by ferry.

Typist: omit "arr" unless related to public transport - & be consistent in all respects throughout.

Outward Tues. 7 Sept			Return Fri. 10 Sept.	
2.47	dep.	Brighton (Platform 1)	arr.	9.37
3.59	arr.	Portsmouth Harbour	dep.	8.08
4.40	dep.	Portsmouth Harbour	arr.	8.00
5.10	arr	Ryde Pier	dep.	7.30

Hovercraft services are available if required

c Some curtailed words: plane, phone, bus, flu.

Inverted commas

Inverted commas are used:

1 To enclose spoken or quoted matter.

2 To represent the sign for inch or inches, as 10".

3 To represent the sign for seconds in geographical measurements, as 69° 10′ 25"N.

4 As a sign for the word *ditto*. (This should be centred under each word to be repeated.)

Note: Single quotes are used when a quoted passage occurs within a quotation or speech, eg The girl replied "I remember his very words: 'I will make good, Mary, I promise you', then he went out and I haven't seen him since." (Some printers, however, reverse the order and use double quotes inside single quotes.)

Punctuation marks should be placed before or after final quotation marks, according to the sense of the sentence. This is the logical style. Some House Rules, however, particularly in printing, require that the final quotation marks are always shown after the punctuation.

The hyphen

The hyphen is used:

1 In compound words as head-dress, hot-house, humming-bird, but the tendency today is to join many of the more commonly established words, and to drop the hyphen, as bedroom, housekeeper, meantime, etc. However, v. para. 5 *infra*.

2 To join compound adjectives as:
This garden has a five-foot wide path.
A never-to-be-forgotten event.
A ten-year-old boy.

Note:

a The difference between:
Six inch nails were used for the work. *and*
Six-inch nails were used for the work.
An old clothes dealer. *and* An old-clothes dealer.

b The use of the hyphen in the following case:
They looked at the flats in two-, three- and four-storey houses.

3 To distinguish between such words as resort and re-sort, recreation and re-creation, recover and re-cover.

4 With the use of some prefixes, as pre-Georgian, non-inductive, ex-Chairman.

5 In some cases to break up an awkward group of vowels or consonants, as co-ordination, co-operation, re-enter, Ross-shire, shell-less, well-known.

6 For dividing words at ends of lines, as com-pare, swim-ming (*see* page 20).

7 To represent the dash (preceded and followed by a space).

8 To represent the minus sign (*see* under 'Dash').

9 In the formation of combination characters as:

+ I̶ = x̶

10 Sometimes to indicate enclosures in letters.

11 To type a 'broken line' indicating perforation as seen in a form at the end of the letter which is filled in and detached.

12 To delete words not required when completing a form. The 'x' may also be used in the same way.

The dash

The dash is used:

1 To add a thought at the end of a sentence:
Miss Scott reappeared to enormous cheering – an indication of her great popularity.

2 To represent a form of parenthesis or apposition (with greater emphasis than the use of commas):
Francis Chichester's feat – the greatest since Francis Drake's in 1577 – was reported all over the world.

3 To indicate that a sentence has been interrupted, or ends suddenly:
'This is the third time I have had to speak to you on this subject and I am – – –' (the girl swept out and banged the door).

4 To indicate hesitating speech:
'Well, I don't know – I – er – yes.'

5 To indicate the omission of a name, or that it is undesirable to print a particular word, whose meaning is derogatory:
The celebrated Lord – was present.
He said he called her a – liar.
In this use, sometimes two preceding and following spaces are used.

6 To represent the minus sign:
6 - 3 = 3; 3 - 6 = -3, that is he was left with a total of -3 (no space after hyphen because this indicates a minus quantity).

7 Before the name of an author following a quotation:
'The secret of success is constancy in purpose' – Disraeli.

Note: The dash separates, and is typed with a space before and after it.

Task 100

Extra note to Typist
Please change times to 24-hour clock

Typist – Mr. Popplethwaite, who is the new Area Manager of Hotels Equipment Co. Ltd. is going on a 4-day visit to the Isle of Wight. Will you please make him out an itinerary according to the following draft. (1+1).
Also a smaller, separate timetable for the outward & return journeys.

Front page

4-Day visit to the Isle of Wight
by Mr. E. P. Popplethwaite, Area Manager
Hotels Equipment Company Ltd. /in full
Itinerary 7th – 10th September, 19..

Tuesday, 7th September

5.10 p.m. arr. Ryde (Accommodation booked at the Pier Hotel for one night)

6.45 p.m. Dinner at Pier Hotel with Mr. E. May (President of Hotels Assoc.)

Wednesday, 8th September

10.00 am The Old Castle, Ryde
Manageress: Miss F. Hepworth

11.30 a.m. Appointment, at The Old Castle, with Mr. F. Croad (Rep. of J. Black & Co.)

12.15 p.m. Lunch at Pussers Hotel with Mr. Croad & Mr. R. Brett (Manager of Black & Sons)

2.45 p.m. dep. Ryde, by car, with Mr. May, who will accompany you ~~round~~ on your visits.

3.30 p.m. arr. Rock Hotel, Sandown
Manager: Mr. H. Lewis

4.45 p.m. The Winslow Restaurant, Sandown
Proprietor: Mr. M. Maggs

7.00 p.m. arr. Dinner at Cliff Hotel, Shanklin (Accom. booked for one night)
Manager: Mr. J. Hayward

(continued)

The underscore (underline)

The underscore is used:

1 For subject headings in letters, titles in literary work, etc. It may be better to retain it under lower-case characters.

2 For indicating to the printer that the word/s underscored should be in italics.

3 For the making of ruled lines under columns of figures, and for double total lines.

4 For ruling across the page when required in forms, before footnotes in literary work, etc.

5 For ruling in tabular work, ornamental borders, etc.

6 For authorities at the end of quotations.

Underscoring should begin under the first letter of the words to be underscored, and finish under the last letter. Final punctuation is usually *not* underscored.

Using an electronic typewriter or a word processor this function is carried out automatically.

Exclamation marks

An exclamation mark is used:

1 Following an obvious exclamation: Oh, dear!

2 To indicate surprise or an implied impression:
So Jane was offered the post – and I thought she was a failure!

3 After a sentence containing *what* or *how* in exclamatory form:
What an improvement! How attractive that looks!

4 Inversions and omissions of words and wishes:
Much good may it do you! Not at all! A great help you have been!

5 As a device in parenthesis for calling attention to a humorous or ironical situation:
She said she really loved (!) being ill.

Note: Spacing after an exclamation mark at the end of a sentence is the same as for a full stop.

In poetry, in the course of a sentence, one space only, and followed by a small letter.

'. . . O Youth! for years so many and sweet
'Tis known that thou and I were one . . ."
– S T Coleridge

Brackets

Brackets are used:

1 To enclose part of a sentence in parenthesis:
The new Beauty Queen (who was crowned yesterday) has agreed to give a Press interview.

Note: Punctuation is placed inside or outside according to meaning and sense.

2 To enclose an authority, reference or translation.

3 To enclose interpolations and remarks made by the writer of the text.

4 To enclose, in the report of a speech, interruptions by the audience, as (applause), (laughter), etc.

5 To enclose reference letters or figures that classify statements (1), (a).

Note: This can be written with the right hand bracket only, as 1), *a*). Two or three spaces usually follow the bracket.

6 In the formation of the brace (*see* page 21).

Note: A further use of brackets is to enclose (*sic*) in the text, meaning that the wording has been copied exactly, though it may be wrong.

Square brackets are used:

a In a quoted passage to indicate corrections, comments, etc., which do not appear in the original.
b In the report of a speech, comments made by the writer and not the speaker.
c To indicate a missing or mis-spelt word.
d As outer brackets, when both types occur together:
e.g. . . . [Here the author contradicts herself (*see* page 38)] . . .

Inside 2 pages

Enjoy a day out à la française

BOULOGNE is a particularly attractive town + boasts one of the busiest seaports in France.

caps/ Boulogne has an excellent shopping centre with a hypermarket f. the ideal shopping spree.

Boulogne holds a colourful market f. local vegetables, cheeses + flowers every Saturday.

BOULOGNE has a large number of restaurants where a variety of gourmet dishes can be enjoyed, so pleasant when in the real French company –

C'est l'ambiance qui compte!

Boulogne can be enjoyed by just ^walking around + mixing with the French inhabitants – + why not try out yr own expertise in the language? The French take pleasure in talking to visitors, especially when they make the effort to talk in French.

Your entitlement to wines, spirits + cigarettes will be given to you in a separate leaflet.

Venez nous joindre pour la journée

BOULOGNE is a town of contrasts – you can enjoy the shopping centre ^+ museum or savour the old town atmosphere in one of the many cafés + visit the Haute Ville with the Cathedral of Notre Dame.

Rule up in pencil for photos

4 cm	11 cm

Le Marché

4 cm	11 cm

La Vieille Ville

caps ‖ Make this a real social occasion f. the members of our French Clubs.

If we all wear blue, white + red lapel badges recognition will be easy.

Au 21 juin!

Punctuation Tasks – Copying

When typing the following tasks special attention should be paid to the correct use of punctuation and use of capital letters.

Task 5 *a* The Beauty of England

When I think of the most beautiful English scenery – and for England the most beautiful means not the grand (which is in the North), but the rich and soft and the sunny – I usually think of Devonshire. But on reflection I feel that the prize is not so easily won. After a week in Herefordshire I am satisfied that there cannot, anywhere in England, be scenery so appealingly lovely. My last tour through it remains with me as an impression of black-and-white villages and towns; of orchards, and by implication, Hereford cider; of the Golden Valley (or valley of the little Dore); of frustrated efforts to see another hamlet which I have long wished to see – England's Gate; of the Black Mountains; Offa's Dyke (the remains nothing so impressive as Hadrian's Wall); the Wye, which is with you in so many parts of the county; and, one upon another, gardens, gardens, gardens.

England is a land of sweet gardens and of garden literature; and so varied are the gardens that it is almost futile to attempt to judge between them. Each has its own law and justification. Yet, somewhat rashly, I am prepared to say that I have seen none to compare with these Herefordshire gardens, and if in the past I said the same about the gardens of the Upper Thames, and later may say the same about some of the Isle of Wight gardens, that is not because I am fickle, but because of England's richness of gardens. There are the gardens of the great, usually open to the public at a small fee, which goes to the local hospital; there are the gardens of the smaller country house; there are the gardens of the middle-class country villa, and the cottage gardens of the peasantry; and all are glorious.

– Thomas Burke

b "Business cannot be done on purely altruistic principles; neither do I think that the principle of 'service' appeals generally; it is too ideal and one-sided; but 'mutual benefit' is practical two-sided business, and will appeal to all if we only open our eyes to it. Our best business men are already adopting this principle, though perhaps not with full consciousness, and finding that it works admirably all round."

Task 6

"What might London have been if, even in the time of our own memories, development could have been guided so as to spare its beauties and antiquities, while planning and tidying up in between! In the last generation, beyond minor losses too many to be numbered, we have destroyed Crosby Hall, the one example in London of a great City merchant's dwelling of the Middle Ages; Newgate, probably the most expressive work of architecture by a follower of Wren in England; the old Post Office in St. Martin's-le-Grand, a dignified public building of most careful workmanship; the school of Christ's Hospital, a pleasant old building of red brick, and original of the type architects have been imitating; the delightful row of houses, attributed to Inigo Jones, in Great Queen Street; the Rolls Chapel, a XIIIth century treasure and some of the City churches."

Task 7

This task illustrates the correct use of capital letters.

A verdict of Death from Natural Causes was returned.

In the Congregational Church at Longmore the congregational singing is superb.

The Duke of Montrose is to move the Address in the House of Lords at the opening of Parliament.

The incidents I have related occurred about a year after the date of the end of the Second World War.

The ancient Hall of Clifford's Inn is one of the few remaining links with the London that survived the Great Fire.

The Government and the leaders of the Opposition are agreed as to the reply to be sent in answer to the Note of the Powers.

Task 8

"We are in the following lines of business, every one of which grows out of the making of motors: aeroplanes, coal mining, coke manufacture, car, truck and tractor manufacture, glass manufacture, artificial leather, copper wire, Fordite, textiles, batteries and generators, paper, cement, automobile bodies, Johanssen gauges, electric power, filtered water, flour, motion pictures, hospital farming and stock raising, radio, printing, photography, forging, flax growing, steam turbine, electric locomotives, logging, saw mills, body parts, dry kilns, wood distillation, products of hydro-electric power, grocery stores, show stores, clothing stores, butcher's shop, railroads, educational, ocean transportation, lake transportation, tractors and automobiles."

– Henry Ford

Task 99

Typist – a) Please type this as a 4-page leaflet.
b) Memo to Mr J. Fraser, enclosing leaflet for him to check. Suggest copies be sent to all Anglo-French Clubs within easy reach of Folkestone. Will phone him tomorrow afternoon to discuss. (From: Miss R. Stripp)

Front page

ANGLO – FRENCH SOCIETY

DAY EXCURSION

TO

BOULOGNE

Via Folkestone

—

Saturday 21 June 19..

—

Organise your own party –
and make it an opportunity to meet Members from other Clubs – & enjoy a day in France together.

Back page

TRAVEL ARRANGEMENTS

Full details concerning travel arrangements, fares & passports are given in the attached leaflet

(continued)

Task 9

"Ham carrying me on his back and a small box of ours under his arm, and Peggotty carrying another small box of ours, we turned down lanes bestrewn with bits of chips and little hillocks of sand, and went past gasworks, ropewalks, boatbuilders' yards, ship-wrights' yards, ship-breakers' yards, caulkers' yards, riggers' lofts, smiths' forges, and a great litter of such places, until we came out upon the dull waste I had already seen at a distance; when Ham said: 'Yon's our house, Mas'r Davy!' "

– *David Copperfield*

Task 10

"Very true," said the Duchess; "flamingoes and mustard both bite. And the moral of that is – 'Birds of a feather flock together'."

"Only mustard isn't a bird," Alice remarked.

"Right, as usual," said the Duchess; "what a clear way you have of putting things!"

"It's a mineral, I *think*," said Alice.

"Of course it is," said the Duchess, who seemed ready to agree to anything that Alice said; "there's a large mustard-mine near here. And the moral of that is – 'The more there is of mine, the less there is of yours'."

"Oh, I know!" exclaimed Alice, who had not attended to this last remark, "it's a vegetable. It doesn't look like one, but it is."

– *Alice in Wonderland*

Task 11

For three days and nights we steered on the cloud over Angatau; the weather was brilliant, the oar alone held us on our course, and the current played us no tricks. On the fourth morning Torstein relieved Herman after the 4–6 watch and was told that Herman thought he had seen the outlines of a low island in the moonlight. When the sun rose just afterwards, Torstein stuck his head in at the cabin door and shouted –

"Land ahead!"

We all plunged out on deck, and what we saw made us hoist all our flags. First the Norwegian aft, then the French at the masthead because we were heading for a French colony. Soon the raft's entire collection of flags was fluttering in the fresh trade wind – the American, British, Peruvian and Swedish flags, besides the flag of the Explorers' Club, so there was no doubt on board that now the "Kon-Tiki" was dressed. The island was ideally placed this time, right in our own course, and a little farther away from us than Puka-puka had been when it cropped up at sunrise four days before. As the sun rose straight up over the sky astern of us, we could see a clear green glimmer high up towards the misty sky over the island. It was the reflection of the still green lagoon on the inside of the surrounding reef. Some of the low atolls throw up mirages of this kind for many thousand feet into the air, so that they show their position to primitive seafarers many days before the island itself is visible above the horizon.

– *The Kon-Tiki Expedition* by Thor Heyerdahl

Insertion of Punctuation

Type the following tasks, insert all necessary punctuation, capital letters and paragraphs, and display to the best advantage.

Task 12

Im a circus man sir my brother and I have our own show that must be an interesting life but surely you must have some knowledge of maths to attend to the business side well sir my sister does all that you see sir I mostly show the animals then my brother dick and I train the new acts and supervise the running of the show my young brother whos now in the army shows the horses we had forty head of horses but Im mostly concerned with the lions and my sister does all the secretarial side I went to school of course when I was a kid but since then Ive had no need for maths you see and Ive mostly forgotten what I learnt but I thought seeing that Ive driven a car and a lorry and a tractor that Id take pretty quickly to an aeroplane and I thought that really my work ought to help me a bit youve got to be pretty quick off the mark with the lions and I think Id do well in an aeroplane I really do sir I think that you probably would but not perhaps as a pilot a pilot must know many things which may not come at all easily to you how would you like to be an air gunner very much sir but Id like if you dont mind to be a pilot Im afraid with your lack of mathematical knowledge you will never become a pilot but sir you can allow me to take a three months instructional course if youll give me that chance thats all I ask in three months Ill learn the maths youll learn maths in three months Im afraid its not as easy as that but sir I can train a complete new act in three weeks Im certain I could do maths in three months give me that chance sir and let me try for a moment the examiners conferred with each other and then the officer said very well have your three months come back after that and well see what you can do then if you are still unsuitable for a pilot you may then like to go as an air gunner oh I would sir id be an air gunner then sir but I think Ill be all right next time thank you sir

– *High Endeavour* by Edward Seago

Task 98

Typist

The Chairman has been called to Manchester to attend a special Board Meeting - will you please make out a timetable for him to take (use A5 folded) and head the front cover:

Flights London and Manchester
and date

From London	hrs	From Manchester	hrs
Car from home	0745	Car to Airport	1500
Heathrow		Airport	
(Flight BE4066)	0835	(Flight BE4095)	1600
Manchester	0925	Heathrow	1645
Car to Phantom House			
Board Meeting	1030		

Task 13

Display carefully, make use of brackets, colon, and dash, etc. Messrs. Reeder & Field, booksellers, Charing Cross Road, WC2H 0BJ dear sirs, I shall be glad if you will dispatch to me one copy of each of the following books
Reconstruction, M. Fanshawe, Allen & Unwin £10.95
International social progress, G A Johnstone Allen & Unwin £12.25
The worlds industrial parliament, E M Oliver
Champions of peace, H Spanes, Allen & Unwin
You will notice that I have not been able to state the name of the publisher in every instance and as I do not know all the prices I am unable to enclose cheque. If you will let me know the total cost I will send a cheque by return yours faithfully

Task 14

messrs watkins & pryde ventnor i w dear sirs as large users of electric lamps the enclosed price list should be of particular interest to you a comparison of our prices with those charged by other firms will show how great an economy can be effected by buying our lamps they are of the best manufacture and for quality are in every way comparable with the best english made lamp any defective lamp will immediately be replaced or credited we carry a large stock and can meet your demands at any time we shall be pleased to quote for any special lamps to meet your requirements and these can be supplied at short notice we can quote you special discounts for large quantities and shall be pleased to supply samples we hope you will let us have a trial order yours faithfully enc

Task 15

a while theres life theres hope he cried

b on approaching the old man we my sister and I noticed that he was reading loves labours lost

c the chairs for the accounts department arrived after a long delay at two oclock yesterday

d as regards business in other directions he said the attractions for speculative activity are not very pronounced.

13 Travel and Dinner Arrangements

It is often necessary for a typist/secretary to make the arrangements for her employer when he goes away to conferences.

She needs to book accommodation well in advance and to plan appointments in co-operation with him.

When typing the *timetables and itineraries*, it is advisable to keep them to a convenient size, and if possible on thin card, so that they can be kept in a wallet. Details for any particular conferences or interviews can be on larger paper, as they may be clipped to files. The amount of detail on itineraries, etc. will depend on individual requirements.

It also comes within the sphere of the typist/secretary, to arrange and organize functions such as conferences and dinners. When names are to be typed in *alphabetical order*, the surname should always appear first, followed by a comma and then the title and initials.

Place names to be put on chairs for reservation purposes should be typed on thin card about $1\frac{1}{2}$ in. by 2 in. in size. The name should be centred, either all in capitals or the surname in capitals, and the whole underlined in red. If a designation is needed, eg the name of the firm being represented, the two lines should be in double spacing and centred on the card. The name only should be underlined. Should the designation take up two lines, these would be in single spacing.

Place names for a dinner table are more attractive if typed on a folded card (about $1\frac{1}{2}$ in. by 3 in. when folded) with the name underlined in red on both sides for easy identification. To ensure a good clean fold the inside of the card should be slightly scored with a knife or pair of scissors. To type on small card, cut slits in a sheet of A4 to take the four corners of the card and repeat so that several can be typed at the same time, or double-fold the paper, towards the top, so that a ledge is formed in which to stand the cards. In each case the cards are fed in from the front.

At some time in a typist's career she will probably be called upon to type a *menu*; this can be produced as a simple display of centring, or can involve some kind of ornamental border (*see* page 96).

In order to save time some restaurants and hotels now have their menus typed in blocked style instead of centring each line.

The following tasks should be displayed attractively, paying due attention to the instructions.

Task 97

Typist The following people have been invited to Speech Day and will take lunch with the Principal beforehand. Please make out the necessary reservation name cards for both these functions.

His Worship the Mayor	The local M.P.	Sir George Bumble
Mr. F. Spreadbury	Mrs. M. Prym	Dr. L. Plunkitt
The Principal of the College		

4 Miscellaneous Information

Division of words at line ends

An operator using an electronic typewriter or a word processor is not concerned with the problems of line-end division of words as these are taken care of automatically. The professional typist, however, using an electric or manual machine, should be able to keep a neat right-hand margin, usually without dividing words at line ends. When this is unavoidable division should be made as near to the end of the word as possible so that the whole word is suggested to the reader. It is better not to divide words on more than two consecutive lines. The following are the generally accepted rules governing the division of words:

Divide:

Between natural syllables: struc-ture, micro-scope, speci-men, engross-ment, immi-grate.

After a prefix: intro-duce, magni-tude, pro-pose. *Note*: prop-erty (because of the pronunciation).

Before a suffix: monu-ment, situa-tion, manage-able, bio-logical.

Between double consonants: syl-lable, neces-sary, excel-lent. *Note*: When the final consonant of the root word is doubled for the addition of a suffix, divide between the repeated consonant, eg swim-ming, run-ning, occur-ring. Exceptions: occurred, preferred (because of pronunciation), *but* pass-ing (ing is added to the root word "pass").

Between two different consonants: finan-cial, moun-tain, win-dow, cur-tain, prac-tice.

In between three consonants: division is usually made after the first, so that the two consonants to be sounded together are not separated, chil-dren, hun-dred, frus-trate, magis-trate.

So that the first letter of the new line is a consonant, where pronunciation permits. Exceptions to this rule are when a suffix or recognized ending begins with a vowel, eg -ing, -able, -ible, -ance, -est, -ish, etc. Cheat-ing, indispens-able, respons-ible, temper-ance, earli-est, self-ish.

Hyphenated words so that they are divided *only* where the hyphen occurs: self-reliant, twenty-six, pre-eminent.

Never divide:

a Proper nouns (Robinson, Manchester).
b The title from initials and name (Mr F Smith).
c Degrees and honorary letters after the name.
d Sets of figures.
e Sums of money or measurements.
f Words of one syllable and their plurals, eg again, match, matches, piece, pieces. (*Note*: exception child – children.)
g When one or two letters would be left on a line, or would be taken over to the new line, eg start(ed) quick(ly) (re)flect.
h The last word of a paragraph or page.

Combination characters

Combination characters are those which are made out of two single characters, typed one over the other. In some cases the interliner has to be used. The main combination characters are as follows:

Typed on the normal line of type:

Brackets (Square)	[ ]	by using the solidus and underscore
Caret	∠	by using the solidus and underscore

Task 96 (continued)

Your directors have already taken steps to enquire into the difficulties being experienced in the S.E. area, & when a full investigation has been made, it is hoped that a solution will be found. (to the problems)

Property Development

Your directors have entered into a contract for the purchase of land adjoining existing premises at the Bolton branch. A

New Plant

The policy of your directors to introduce modern plant whenever possible necessary to ensure the greatest productivity has continued. New machinery was installed in the Norwich branch during the year, & a considerable amount will have to be spent in the equipping of the new premises in Bolton.

Prospects

The past year's trading, although a little disappointing has been on a satisfactory basis. I do not wish to forecast any results for the coming year, but indications are that trading for the current year so far, shows a reasonable increase on the corresponding period of last year. I therefore have every reason to expect that I shall be able to report that a recovery has taken place when I address you next year.

In conclusion I should like to express the thanks of the Board & the Shareholders to all members of the staff who have worked so energetically during the difficult year through which we have just passed.

A (It is anticipated that building will begin within the next three months, as plans have already been passed by the Local Authority.)

Division	÷	by using the colon and hyphen
Dollar	$	by using capital S and solidus
Exclamation mark	!	by using the full stop and apostrophe

Typed in conjunction with the interliner:

*Asterisk	*	by using small x and hyphen
*Dagger	†	by using capital I and hyphen
*Double dagger	‡	by using two capital I's
Equation ('Equals')	=	by using two hyphens
Per cent	%	by using two o's and the solidus
Section	§ s	by using two capital or small S's

The plus sign cannot be satisfactorily made. It is usually written afterwards with a ballpoint pen if not provided on the typewriter. The following are not *combination* characters but are those which fulfil a special function:

Brace	{ or }	by using brackets
Dash	-	a hyphen with a space before and after
Decimal point	13.5	a full stop
Diaeresis	Noël	the quotation sign
Feet	3'	the apostrophe
Inches	7"	the quotation sign
Minutes (Geographical)	20'	the apostrophe
Minus	8 - 5	a hyphen with a space before and after
Multiplication	4 x 2	small x with a space before and after
Seconds (Geographical)	25"	the quotation sign
Sloping fraction	2/9	the solidus separating the numerator from the denominator

*These symbols are used in footnotes and are always typed as superior characters (see page 67).

Task 96

Typist –
Please type 1+1

The Eversharp Tools Company Limited u/c

Chairman's Report

In spite of present difficulties I am happy to be able to tell you that yr. Company has ~~made a slight~~ increased its profits during the year. The large capital expenditure which was made two years ago, & which many of you doubted was wise, has proved to be worthwhile. I cannot say that I am altogether satisfied with the results, but many/ other cos. of a similar nature are showing lower profits, so that, considering the general state of world markets, I feel
¶ we need not be dis-heartened.

In common with many other organisations, the difficulty of obtaining & maintaining an adequate labour force has delays/ caused ~~holdups~~ in production on the one hand, & has increased costs, owing to the necessity of over-time working, on the other hand.

Profits & Dividends

From the a/cs it will be seen that the profits for the year amounted to £50,790 more than last year. After making provision for taxation & transfer to Taxation Equalisation Account, & after deducting the Preference
NP Dividend, there remains a profit of £1,115,650. [As forecast in the Interim Statement, yr. Directors are recommending a final dividend of 6%, which with the Interim dividend already paid, amounts to a total of 12%, which is the same as for the previous year.

It is hoped, & anticipated, that a similar dividend will be possible for the year ahead.

Branches & Subsidiaries

Although there has been a slight falling off in demand for our products in the S.E. area, the Northern branches have shown a slight improvement, & therefore the overall picture has been satisfactory.

(continued)

The interliner is used when typing the following:

Cedilla	ç	a comma slightly lowered and touching c
Degrees	54°	a small o slightly raised
Fraction	$\frac{4}{9}$	the underscore separating the numerator from the denominator

Printers' correction signs

The duties of a secretary or shorthand-typist often include the preparation of 'copy' for the printer and subsequently proof reading and correction. In order to ensure complete accuracy there are standard signs understood by typists and printers alike. The correction is made in the margin, separated from the text by a solidus, and a mark is made at the point where the correction is to be made.

The more important signs are given below; those applicable to both typing and printing first – followed by those applicable to printing only.

Marginal mark	**Meaning**	**Mark in text**	
caps/	Change to caps	≡	under word/s to be in caps (printing)
		≡	under word/s to be in spaced caps (typing)
		=	under word/s to be in small caps (printing)
		=	under word/s to be in closed caps (typing)
uc/ or (cap)	Change to upper case		underline or strike through letter or letters to be altered
lc/ or (small)	Change to lower case		underline or strike through letter or letters to be altered
Para/	New paragraph	[	before first word of new paragraph
NP/	New paragraph	[	before first word of new paragraph
run on/	No new paragraph	⌒	continue previous paragraph
stet/	Leave as originally written	- - - - -	under word/s to be left in
∂/	Delete		Word/s crossed through
trs/	Transpose	⌣	between letter/s or word/s. Word order is indicated by 3 1 2 4.
⁐	Close up, no space	⁐	linking letters or words
∂̑	Delete and close up		Strike out word/s to be deleted, link up words

Task 95

THe GROSVENOR TENNIS CLUB

18 Grosvenor Pk Rd.

Torquay.

Dear Member.

A meeting of th e Grosvenor tennis Club willbe held at the above Premises on Fridy, 2nd. March at 19. 00 hrs.

As this isthe first meeting of teh year, when important decisions will be made, it is hoped you will make every endeavour to bepresent.

A.F. Hurst

Hon. Sec.

Agenda

1.Minutes of the last meeting
2 Matters arising
32.Correspondence and apologies for absence.
3. Treasurer's financial Statement.
4. Arrangements for Summer season
5.Organisation of matches .
6. AOB

Sheila – The secretary of the local Tennis Club wants to have this letter and agenda photo-copied. He has asked me if I could get it properly typed as he is not very good on the typewriter! Would you help out please?

Marginal mark	Meaning	Mark in text	
#	Space required	⋏	between letter or words
eq #	Equal spacing required	/	between letters or words
ital/	Change to italics	___	under word/s to be italicised
words required/	Caret—insert matter indicated in margin	⋏	at point where insertion required
take over	Take over to next line	[	before words to be transferred to next line
take back	Take back to last line	]	before words to be transferred to last line
move	Move matter as indicated	[ ]	around words to be moved
raise	Raise line	↑	at point where line is to be raised
lower	Lower line	↓	at point where line is to be lowered
⊙	Insert full stop	⋏	
(:)	Insert colon	⋏	
;/	Insert semi-colon	⋏	
,/	Insert comma	⋏	
'/	Insert apostrophe	⋏	
'/ '/	Insert single quotes	⋏ or ⋏ ⋏	
"/ "/	Insert double quotes	⋏ or ⋏ ⋏	
|-|	Insert hyphen	⋏	
|—|	Insert dash	⋏	
⊐	Move to left	⊐	at right of words to be moved
⊏	Move to right	⊏	at left of words to be moved
═	Straighten line	═	under line to be straightened
‖	Straighten margin	‖	at point where margin is out of alignment
wf/	Wrong fount		encircle letter/s to be altered
X	Damaged letter		encircle damaged letter
∂	Letter upside down		encircle letter to be altered
sc/	Small caps	═	under word/s to be altered

The Chairman reported on the heavy administrative costs, & after discussion it was agreed that ~~it~~ each member of the Board would look into this matter & report at the next meeting.

5. <u>Completion of Contract with Dawsons Ltd.</u>

Mr. Harris reported on the contract with Dawsons Ltd. & stated that the date for completion should be ~~(by)~~ /known by the end of the week, & that delivery of the first consignment would be within a month of the signing of the contract.

6. <u>AOB</u>

The question of the Annual Works Competition was raised & it was agreed to put this on the agenda for the next meeting.

7. <u>Date of next Meeting</u>

The date of the next meeting was fixed for Tues. 8th June.

Chairman

June 19..

The name of the Liaison Officer was given as Mr H. Levent

<u>Typist</u> The Chairman wants to see how this looks with side headings in the margin - please retype to end of item No. 4 in both block & indented styles.

Roman numerals

There are seven symbols:

Units	I	(1)	Fives	V	(5)
	X	(10)		L	(50)
	C	(100)		D	(500)
	M	(1,000)			

1. Any unit symbol can be repeated two or three times:

I (1)	X (10)	C (100)
II (2)	XX (20)	CC (200)
III (3)	XXX (30)	CCC (300)

2. Any unit or repeated unit may be used after any other symbol of higher value to indicate addition:

VI (6)	XII (12)	LIII (53)	CII (102)	DIII (503)
LX (60)	CXX (120)	DXXX (530)	DC (600)	MCC (1,200)

3. A single *unit* symbol only may be placed before its immediately succeeding 'five' or 'ten' symbol to indicate the subtraction of that single unit from the 'five' or 'ten' unit:

	IV = 4	XL = 40	CD = 400
	IX = 9	XC = 90	CM = 900
Note:	49 = XLIX	99 = XCIX	999 = CMXCIX

4. When changing arabic numerals (2, 3, 4, etc) to roman, each figure has to be taken separately in turn, eg:

789 = 700 = 500 + 200 = DCC
 = 80 = 50 + 30 = LXXX
 = 9 = 10 − 1 = IX
 DCCLXXXIX

5. A line placed over a symbol multiplies it by 1,000 eg $\overline{\text{VI}}$ = 6,000 $\overline{\text{IX}}$ = 9,000.

Use of roman numerals

Large roman numerals are used for:

a Names of monarchs (Elizabeth II).
b Inscription dates (MCMLIX).
c Form numbers in schools.
d Chapter headings and sections.
e Acts in plays.
f Books of the Bible.
g Clock dials (on which four often appears as IIII).
h Enumerating paragraphs when arabic numerals are not convenient.

Small roman numerals are used for:

a Introductory pages of books.
b Appendices.
c Subsidiary paragraphs and clauses.
d Scenes in plays (though arabic numerals are usually preferred).
e Chapters in the Bible (II Samuel iv, 2).

Arabic

1. Arabic numerals are expressed by numbers 1, 2, 3, etc.
2. Cardinal numbers are 1, 2, 3.
3. Ordinal numbers are 1st, 2nd, 3rd (these denote order: they are not abbreviations, and therefore do not need a full stop).

Note: Large roman numerals may be followed by a full stop only when numbering paragraphs or sections.

Enumeration in reports, etc

1. Chapter headings and sections—large roman.
2. Paragraphs—arabic.
3. Clauses or sub-paragraphs—small roman.

Note: All roman numerals (large and small) must keep a strict right- or left-hand margin, according to the style of display adopted.

Typist
Please type in block style

THE HOWARD MANUFACTURING COMPANY LIMITED

Minutes of the meeting of the Board of Directors held at the registered offices of the Company on Tuesday 4th May, 19.. at 11/45 ~~am~~ hrs

Present Mr. F. Drayton in the Chair

Mr. S. Small
Mr. A. Bishop
Mr. F. Fox } Directors
Mr. W. Harris
Mr. B. Williams
Mr. S. Croxley Secretary

1. Minutes

The Minutes of the meeting held on 4th April were read approved & signed.

2. Matters arising

Mr. Bishop reported that the architect was still working on the plans of the new extension.

3. Correspondence

The secretary read letters from Clark & Shaw, Reed & Mann, & Black & Talbot – all ~~regarding~~ in answer to the circular letter sent to them ~~re~~ regarding increased transport costs. 'MANN'

Black & Talbot advised that they were transferring some of their works to Birmingham.

4. Financial statement

The sec. reported that there were still ~~8~~ cheques of over £1000 outstanding & that renewed application had been made to ~~them~~ the firms concerned. [The figure of £2000000 to the Coy's credit was confirmed by the bank statement. /18 NP

Mr. Williams submitted a report on ~~the question of~~ obtaining supplies in an emergency, & the advantages of dealing with a small, reliable, local/ firm. After discussion it was proposed by Mr. Williams, seconded by Mr. Harris & unanimously

RESOLVED: That an account be opened with John Palmers Ltd.

(continued)

Figures and words

The general rule is that in:

Literary work, words should be used for all numbers under 100, for whole numbers, and when a number begins a sentence, but this may vary according to the type of book and the 'House Rules' of individual publishers.

Correspondence, figures are used more frequently because they are clearer and are more easily grasped.

Legal work, numbers are written out in words, often with the figures in brackets (*see* page 160).

Common sense, consistency and the nature of the work must be the deciding factors in the use of words and figures, but the following general points should be noted:

Use words:

a For the number 'one' on its own, numbers 'two' to nine inclusive in general work, and numbers under 100 in literary work.
b When the number is expressed in an indefinite way, eg There were about four hundred people present.
We have driven nine or ten miles.
c When referring to population or quantity, eg My home town has over ten thousand inhabitants.
Because of the weather, only sixty per cent of the expected audience came to the meeting.
d When a sentence begins with a number, eg One thousand two hundred books were catalogued.
e For measurements, eg The box measured 4 ft. 2 in. square.
f For degrees of heat, eg It was 25°C in the hall.
is now six o'clock.

Use figures:

a When clarity is essential: all in figures, figures after 'one', or from 10 onwards in general work, and for large numbers, and expressions of money.
b For dates, eg 28 February, 1972.
c For distances, eg They drove 15 miles yesterday.
d For weights, eg Their baby weighed 8 lb. 8 oz.
e For measurements, eg The box measured 4ft. 2in. square.
f For degrees of heat, eg It was 25°C in the hall.
g For votes, eg He gained 29,500 votes.
h For house numbers, eg 27 High Street.
i For numbers in postal districts or codes, eg London, W1N 3AP, Croydon CR9 1QH.
j For expressing time using am and pm and the 24-hour clock, eg They are comign at 10 am (1000 hrs.) and leaving at 5 pm (1700 hrs.).
k For numbering policies or certificates, eg PN 75342.
l With the % sign, eg These societies give 7% interest.
m After the abbreviation No for number, eg He has ticket No 67.
n For scores in games and matches, eg England scored 189 runs.

Use words and figures:

In cheques, estimates, legal and other documents where it is essential to ensure accuracy or to prevent the possibility of fraudulent alteration, eg The rental to be paid in equal weekly instalments of fifteen pounds fifty (£15.50). We agree to accept your estimate of £250 (two hundred and fifty pounds) for carrying out the repairs.

Note: Avoid mixing words and figures, 10 thousand – type 10,000 or ten thousand. It is accepted however in very large sums of money, £296 million.

Methods of correcting errors

In the typewriter:

1. The carriage is moved to the side (so that rubber dust does not fall into the type-basket).
2. The cylinder is turned up three or four spaces.
3. A shield or piece of paper is used to protect the copy from finger marks.
4. The erasure is made gently with the side of the rubber.
5. The work is returned to its former alignment and the correction is made.

In the typewriter (half-space method):

This method of correcting is used when it is necessary to substitute a word containing one more letter (or one less) than the word erased. This means that the spacing on either side of the word corrected will be half a space less, or more.

Task 93

Miss Noggin / This is last year's Notice of Meeting please amend with the following information: Date of 65th AGM - Friday 25 October Two Directors to be elected (retiring) Mr. A. G. Black and Mr. J. E. Jones To declare the re-appointment of Titchfield and Barker as Auditors.

THE ALPHA BUILDING SOCIETY

Alpha House,
Cromwell Road,
LEICESTER.
LE2 6ES

ANNUAL GENERAL MEETING

NOTICE IS HEREBY GIVEN that the Sixty-fourth ANNUAL GENERAL MEETING of the Society will be held at Alpha House, Cromwell Road, Leicester, on Friday, 17 October, 19.. at 1930 hrs. for the purpose of transacting the following business:

1. To receive the Directors' Report and Statement of [Accounts for the year ended 30 September, 19..

2. To receive the Auditors' Report.

3. To elect two Directors:

   The following Directors retire from office, and [being eligible offer themselves for re-election - Mr. R. Jacobs and Mr. S. P. Tripp.

4. To elect Auditors.

By Order of the Board

E. B. DODDS

7 October, 19.. Secretary

NOTE: Every member of the Society entitled to attend and vote at the above meeting is entitled to appoint a proxy to attend and vote instead of him. A proxy need not be a member of the Society. Any instrument appointing a proxy must be lodged at the Registered Office of the Society not less than 48 hours before the time appointed for the meeting.

Most typewriters have a special key for half-space correcting, but where this is not fitted the result may be obtained by one of the following methods:

1. Using the back spacer.

2. Using the space bar.

If, for example, the word 'those' is to replace the word 'that', first, the erasure is made. Then:

1. Using the back spacer:

a The carriage is moved to where the second letter had been typed.
b The back spacer is held right down and the first letter is typed, then the back spacer is released.
c One space is tapped, the back spacer is held down again and the second letter is typed.
d Each subsequent letter is dealt with in the same manner.

2. Using the space bar:

a The carriage is moved one space to the left of where the first letter had been typed (ie into the space).
b The space bar is held down and the first letter is typed, then the space bar is released.
c The space bar is again held down while the second letter is typed, and is then released.
d Each subsequent letter is dealt with in the same way.

To replace a four-letter word by one of three letters, the procedure is as above, but to begin, the printing point should be placed where the third letter had been typed if using the back spacer and where the first letter had been typed if using the space bar. This will mean that there will be one and a half spaces instead of the usual one before and after the word corrected.

In the typewriter with carbon copies:

1. The carriage is moved to the side and the cylinder is turned up three or four line spaces.

2. A piece of paper is inserted between each carbon and its copy, to prevent smudging.

3. Each copy is erased separately (a pencil rubber may also be used where necessary).

4. The pieces of paper should be removed when all erasures are completed.

After removal from the typewriter:

1. Erasures and corrections should be carried out separately on each copy.

2. Care must be taken to ensure perfect alignment when the typescript is re-inserted into the machine (top copy and carbons must be corrected separately).

3. In order to obtain the same depth of print on a carbon copy, a carbon is put between the copy and the ribbon at the printing point, once the position for the correction has been ascertained, and then the correction is typed.

After the typescripts have been fastened together (backward feed):

'Backward feed' refers to the insertion of paper into the machine from the front of the cylinder instead of in the normal way. This method of paper insertion is used when a correction or an addition is required on a typewritten sheet fastened at the top to other sheets.

The method of insertion is as follows:

1. A single sheet of paper is inserted into the machine as usual (turning down about two inches).

2. The *bottom* of the typewritten sheet to be corrected (print facing forward) is inserted between this single sheet and the cylinder.

3. The cylinder is turned backwards and the single sheet is removed.

4. The typewritten sheet (with the erasure already made) is then ready for adjustment and correction, by means of the paper release lever, variable line spacer and alignment scale.

Re-insertion:

The paper is fed into the typewriter until the line containing the error is flush with the line gauge. Using the paper release lever, the paper is moved sideways until the characters fall exactly over the scale degrees. The carriage is then moved to the required point opposite the type-bar fork.

Automatic correction and correction liquid and paper

Electronic typewriters and word processors have inbuilt, automatic correction keys, removing the problems of manual correction of errors.

Where such machines are not available, the typist can use correction liquid or paper, or an eraser. A good eraser is probably the best, but takes time; the liquid and paper are quick to use, but the corrections are clearly visible when the typescript is held up to

Task 92

Typist a) Will you prepare the following agenda, please.
b) Agenda for Chairman - extra notes at foot of page

THE CANTHAVEN HORTICULTURAL SOCIETY

Committee Meeting to be held at Andrew House Cathedral Square, Canterbury, on Friday, 28th January 19.. at 8 p.m.

AGENDA

Add No. 5 Sec. Report
No. 6 Treas. Report - a reminder

1. Apologies for absence
2. Minutes of last Meeting
3. Matters arising
4. Correspondence
7 ~~8.~~ Spring Flower Show
(i) General arrangements
(ii) Stewards
(iii) Entries
(iv) awards
6 ~~6.~~ Autumn Flower Show
(i) Report from Chairman on
(iii) last year's show
(ii) Recommendations for next show
5 ~~7.~~ "Any Questions" Evening - election of Sub-Committee
8. AOB
9. Date of next meeting

Notes for Chairman

a.) Mr. S. Manton leaving district (Apologies)
b) Suggest Mr. Bill Sawyer & Miss Freda Luck (Any Questions)
c) Spring Flower Show: (1) Suggest later date, last year too early (2) More publicity needed.
d) Next meeting - suggest end of next month.

the light, and the 'powder' of the correction paper tends to rub off leaving an over-type!

In work to be photocopied, correction liquid for small deletions is ideal; for an extensive correction, it is preferable to paste a strip of paper over the incorrect area and retype.

Carbons

Whilst a variety of carbons is still available, carbons are used, in the main, for file copies (or in conjunction with special machines), as photocopies of an original produce better quality copies for distribution purposes. The following points, however, should be studied.

One-time carbons refer to thinly coated carbons intended for use once only, as in stencilling.

Backed carbon paper refers to a special substance used for the backing of the carbon sheet, thus rendering it easier to handle and less likely to curl. There are also various makes of carbon made of a plastic material, which gives longer life and prevents marking and curling.

NCR (no carbon required) was patented by the National Cash Register Company Limited. In order to obtain a carbon copy without the use of a carbon, the back of the top copy and the front of the flimsy are specially treated, one with crystals, the other with chalk. When pressure is applied, the crystals are crushed and the carbon properties are released. NCR is used particularly in the preparation of invoices.

Weight. Heavy weight carbon gives up to two copies, medium weight gives up to five copies and light weight gives over five copies.

Colours. Black, purple, blue, green, brown and red. These are used for the following purposes:

a To differentiate between copies being sent to different departments.
b To draw attention to certain parts of a document.
c In order to match the ribbon.

Choice of carbons. In choosing the kind of carbon to use, the following points should be taken into consideration: the number of copies required, the type of paper to be used, the performance of the typewriter and the colour required.

Insertion of carbons. When requiring a number of carbon copies an easy method of assembly is to insert the top copy and flimsies into the machine until they are just gripped by the roller, the sheets are folded back individually and the carbons are inserted.

For good copies:
a Type-faces should be in good condition and perfectly clean.
b Platen should be in good condition (not pitted).
c Medium platen is required for up to five copies, hard platen for more than five copies.
d Even touch should be used when typing.
e A backing sheet should be used if one carbon copy only is required.
f A corner should be cut off the top left-hand side of carbons, so that they fall out when the copies are held by this corner and shaken after typing. This ensures clean copies. A number of manufacturers do, in fact, prepare their carbons in this way.
g Carbons should be carefully stored, so that they do not crease.

Varieties of carbons. In addition to the above, special carbons are obtainable for use with the following duplicating processes:
Hectograph – a hectograph carbon is specially produced.
Spirit duplication – specially prepared carbons (transfer sheets) in a variety of colours are available.

'Treeing' is a term used to indicate the tree-like marks on a carbon copy, caused by the carbon being creased.

Stencils, masters and photocopies

Stencil packs are made up with one-time, or double-sided coated carbon. When preparing a stencil the type keys should be quite clean and the ribbon mechanism should be switched to 'stencil', to take it out of action, so that the type keys can hit the stencil directly. A firm rhythmic touch is needed and the stencil should always be checked before being removed from the typewriter.

The use of the duplicator has been largely replaced by the offset-litho process, which approximates to printing. Most offices, however, use the photocopying method of reproduction, as this is quicker and produces better quality reproductions at no greater cost.

Task 91

THE HOWARD MANUFACTURING COMPANY LIMITED

BOARD MEETING

to be held at the Offices of the Company

on Tuesday, ~~6~~ 4/th. May 19.. at 1145 hrs.

Typist Would you retype this agenda for the chairman please? I gave it to one of the juniors and she hasn't a clue!

AGENDA

1. Minutes of the last Meeting.

Secretary to read Minutes of Meeting held on 4th. April.
Sign when confirmed.

2. Matters arising

Possible query regarding the plans for extension building.

3. Correspondence

i) Ask Secretary to deal with this.
ii) Query letter from Messrs. Black & Talbot re change of address.

4. Financial Statement

i) Secretary to give report.
ii) Ask Mr. Williams to explain the opening of an account with John Palmers, Ltd.
iii) Can we make any economies?

5. Completion of Contract with Dawsons, Ltd.

i) Is the date fixed?
ii) Delivery dates - has anything been discussed?
iii) Who is their Liaison Officer?

6. Any other Business.

7. Date of next meeting

Confirm 8th. June, as usual.

Corrections on stencils

Small corrections are made with correcting fluid, that part of the stencil to be corrected being raised slightly before the liquid is applied. Whilst this dries the previous part of the stencil can be checked. When typing in the correct word/s care must be taken to give additional pressure to cut through the extra thickness of wax.

If an extensive correction is to be made, 'grafting' will be necessary. This is a term used to indicate an extensive correction on a stencil by means of patching, when the use of correcting fluid is inadequate. That part of the stencil containing the wrong words is cut out with a small, sharp blade, and part of another stencil is inserted in its place and fixed by means of correcting fluid. Care must be taken to obtain correct alignment, when making the alteration.

'Offset'

This is a term used to indicate that the inked impression from one duplicated sheet has been transferred to the back of another. The remedy is to interleave with used paper until the surplus ink has been absorbed.

Spirit Masters

To produce a master copy for use on a spirit duplicator, a coloured transfer sheet is required, the shiny surface of both the papers being face to face, and the typing taking place on the dull surface of the master. A very even touch is necessary. Corrections are made by using a special eraser, an ordinary soft rubber, or a pen-knife.

Definitions

Alignment

A term used to refer to the typing of words in a straight line. If any character appears above or below the normal line of type, and the line at the base of the characters is uneven, then it is said to be out of alignment.

Backward feed

Refers to the insertion of paper into the machine from the front of the cylinder instead of in the normal way (*see* page 26).

Break line

The last line of a paragraph, if a short line.

Catchword

This is a term used to indicate that there is a continuation sheet. The first word, or words, of the second page is typed at the foot of the first page, two line spaces down from the body, preceded by the solidus, and ending flush with the right hand margin. Catchwords, however, are seldom used.

Dead key

This is a term given to a key which, when struck, does not move the carriage forward the usual one space. (This is because the type-bar has been disconnected from the universal bar.) A dead key, which is usually fitted with an accent for use when typing foreign languages, is struck first, followed by the key with the letter over which the accent is to appear on the typescript.

Draft

1. *To draft*—to prepare or formulate the first rough copy of a letter or document.
2. *A draft*—the first rough copy of any document when in manuscript. When typewritten it should be in double or treble spacing with wide side margins to allow for extensive revision. The word 'DRAFT' should appear at the top left-hand side.
3. *A draft*—applicable mainly to correspondence—the typing of a letter to see how it would fit on to a page in its final form.
4. *Draft*—a legal document, sent between solicitors for approval or amendment, and from which the Engrossment is made.

Dropped head

The term given to the typing of titles and chapter headings lower on the page than usual (allowing a top margin of about $2\frac{1}{2}$ in. instead of 1 in).

Fair copy

The corrected and neatly typed copy of a rough draft, usually in double spacing.

Fit

The term used to indicate that a manuscript divided for typing among several people, will be continuous when the whole is collected together. If the work is divided into chapters, complete chapters will be given to each typist, but if the matter is continuous, it must be divided into sections that will make a definite number of complete pages.

12 Committee Work

To become conversant with committee *procedure* the secretary needs to study and to have experience. The typing connected with committee work, however, is straightforward to the good typist who knows the general display for the various aspects of the work.

Agendas

'Ordinary' agenda. Unless an organisation has its own special display, an Agenda is centred on A5 or A4 paper, whether the format is wholly centred or blocked. The name of the organisation, type of meeting, place, date and time are given, together with a numbered list of items to be discussed, in single spacing, double between items. It is usual to begin with Apologies for absence, Minutes of the last meeting, Matters arising, and Correspondence, and to end with Any other business and Date of next meeting, with the 'business' between.

Chairman's agenda

The style is similar to an ordinary agenda, except that the items are typed with an inch left-hand margin and occupy only the left-hand side of an A4 page, leaving the right for the Chairman's comments. Extra items under the numbered ones may be added for his guidance. Brackets, typed at the same point down the page, or item numbers repeated on the right, separate the two sides.

Agenda incorporated with a letter

A letter is sometimes sent to members, inviting them to a meeting, and adding the agenda within the letter, or following the Secretary's signature.

If the Secretary is not to *sign* the letter, his name will be typed in full capitals in the space normally occupied by the signature.

The notification of an Annual General Meeting sent by a public body such as a Building Society is very formal and is always in the same style (*see* page 136).

A form of proxy is sent out either at the same time as the notification of the meeting, or can be applied for, to enable absent members to vote.

A report is typed in single spacing, or double if required for easy reading.

Minutes of a meeting are either handwritten in a bound book, or are typewritten on loose-leaf sheets and subsequently kept in a safe place.

The heading for minutes, like the agenda, contains the name of the organisation, type of meeting, place, date, time, followed by the list of those present (Chairman first and secretary last), and the items, according to the order on the agenda. Each separate matter discussed (or minute) is numbered for easy reference. The word '*Resolved*' is typed in capitals and the resolutions follow, typed as inset paragraphs.

Minutes are displayed in two forms, either with headings underscored as shoulder heads typed at the margin, or with marginal headings in capitals at 1 in. and main margin set about 3 in.

Study and type these terms and their meanings:

Committee meeting terms

Ad hoc. 'Arranged for this purpose.' An ad hoc sub-committee is one appointed to carry out a specific task.
Amendment. A proposal to alter a resolution under discussion, before it has been adopted.
Any other business (*AOB*). The item under which, at the end of a meeting, any business not already dealt with in the agenda may be discussed.
Casting Vote. The vote given by the Chairman in the event of an equal number of votes being cast 'for' and 'against' a motion.
Convene. To call a meeting.
Co-option. Powers given to a committee to elect individuals on to the committee – usually for specific purposes.
Ex-officio. 'By virtue of office' – a member eligible to serve on one committee by virtue of his office on another.
In Camera. A meeting held in private.
Motion. The formal proposal put to a meeting, which must be proposed, seconded, voted upon, and passed by the majority.
Nem. Con. 'No one contradicting.' No votes have been cast against the motion, though some members may have abstained from voting.
Proxy. A person authorized to vote in place of another.
Quorum. The minimum number of members needed to constitute a meeting, as laid down in the constitution.
Resolution. The formal decision taken at a meeting. It must be proposed, seconded and passed.

Note: The following must be the same for all typists:

1. Type-face.
2. Size of type (elite/pica).
3. Quality and size of paper, colour of ribbon.
4. Width of margins, depth of line spacing, method of numbering and position of page numbers, together with the same method of punctuation.

Hook-in

A term used in connection with poetry, when there are too many words to go on one line, and those at the end are placed above or below it to finish at the same point.

Inferior characters

These are typed half a space below the normal line of type, as in chemical formulae by means of the interliner using the half-space mechanism, eg H_2SO_4, H_2O.

Justifying

The term 'justifying a margin' refers to the spacing of words in a line to ensure a completely even right-hand margin.

Matching in

This is the process of filling in form letters so that the added particulars match the density and colour of the ink impression.

Matching up

The 'matching up' process means the adjusting of the paper so that the characters appear in correct alignment vertically and horizontally, when a completed piece of typescript has to be reinserted to make a correction.

Pagination

The method of numbering pages. Prefaces and preliminary material are usually indicated by small roman numerals, whilst the main part of the content is paginated with arabic numbers. These may be at the left-hand margin, centred or at the right-hand margin, generally 4 line spaces from the top of the page.

In some documents pages are indicated as '6 of 10' indicating that this is page 6 and that there are 10 pages in the whole of a particular piece of work. In plays, the Act and scene may be indicated as well as the page, as shown in this example 'I–4–64'.

Pitch

A term which refers to the spacing on the type-writer, ie the space occupied by each individual character. (The pitch is 10 characters to the inch with pica, and 12 with elite.)

Rubric

A written instruction to be observed when dealing with following matter.

Short page

A term used to indicate that the last page of a document is only partly filled, eg at the end of a chapter.

Superior characters

These are typed half a space above the normal line of type, by means of the interliner or using the half space mechanism, as in algebraic formulae, footnotes, etc.

eg x^2y^3 $50°$ . . . latest book* . . .

Stitching margin

An extra margin of half an inch to allow work to be bound together without any words being obscured. If both sides of the paper are to be used, the extra margin would appear on the left-hand side of odd numbered pages, and on the right-hand side of even numbered pages.

Tail piece

The decoration at the end of a chapter, article or programme.

c) PERCENTAGE BAR CHART

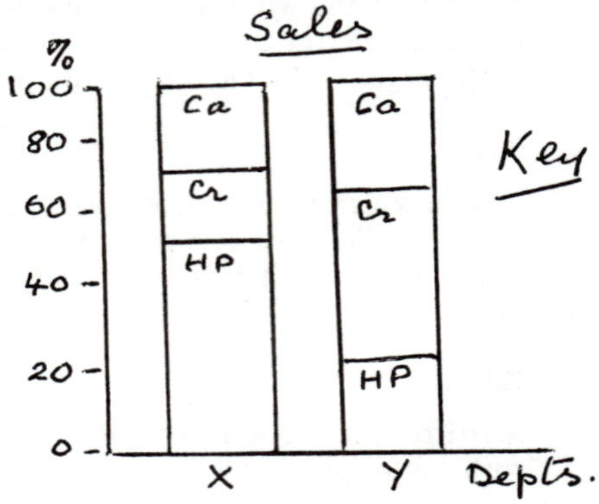

Calculations

X $\frac{6}{22} \times 100 = 27\%$

$\frac{4}{22} \times 100 = 18\%$

$\frac{12}{22} \times 100 = 55\%$

Y $\frac{8}{26} \times 100 = 31\%$

$\frac{12}{26} \times 100 = 46\%$

$\frac{6}{26} \times 100 = 23\%$

This is similar to a Component Bar Chart, except that the information is shown as a percentage.

d) PIE CHART

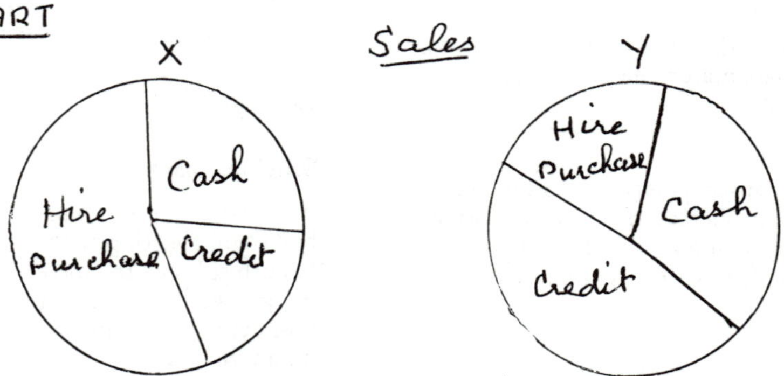

The information is illustrated as a percentage, but of a circle, i.e. 360°

Calculations

Cash	$\frac{6}{22} \times 360° = 98°$		Cash	$\frac{8}{26} \times 360° = 111°$
Cr.	$\frac{4}{22} \times 360° = 65°$		Cr	$\frac{12}{26} \times 360° = 166°$
HP	$\frac{12}{22} \times 360° = 197°$		HP	$\frac{6}{26} \times 360° = 83°$

5 Abbreviations

When drafting a document, abbreviations such as wd, cont, ffy, and sec are permitted, but in its final form, only recognized abbreviations such as eg, ie, viz, NB, etc are used—and these are *never* written out.

Traditionally, abbreviations are followed by a full stop—eg, ie, viz, NB, etc, but nowadays in the interest of speed the full stop is generally omitted, both at the end of and between the letters of the abbreviation, the letters being typed close together. This is called open punctuation (*see* page 14). In some forms the oblique stroke may be replaced by the full stop, eg b.f, b.d.

General work

The following are generally used in their abbreviated form:

eg	(exempli gratia)	for example
etc	(et cetera)	and so on
et seq	(et sequentes)	and the following
ie	(id est)	that is
viz	(videlicet)	namely

(When used in the middle of a sentence, a comma must be typed before the above abbreviations.)

anon		anonymous
cf (cp)	(confer)	compare
ibid	(ibidem)	in the same place
id	(idem)	the same
NB	(nota bene)	mark well, take note
qv	(quod vide)	which see
v	(versus)	against

Manuscripts The following are some of the most common abbreviations used in the preparation of a typescript from manuscript:

del	delete, take out
ital	italics (change to)
lc	lower case (small)
p (pp)	page (s)
par (para)	paragraph
MS (MSS)	manuscript (s)
stet	let it stand, keep in
trs	transpose
uc	upper case (caps)
wf	wrong fount

Courtesy titles When honours, distinctions and academic degrees, etc, follow a person's name, each group should be separated by a space eg F W Green Esq OBE DFC BA FRSA JP (but F. W. Green, Esq., O.B.E. in traditional style).

Commercial Abbreviations. There are a large number of abbreviations which come into this group, but the following are examples of the more general ones:

Co Company Ltd Limited PLC (Plc, plc) Public Limited Company Bros Brothers	These abbreviations should be used only when applied to the names of firms

The following abbreviations may, in certain circumstances, remain in this form:

am	ante meridiem, before noon
c/o	care of
COD	cash on delivery
E & OE	errors and omissions excepted
Enc	enclosure
Hon	Honourable, Honorary
Jun	Junior
M	Monsieur
MM	Messieurs
Mme	Madame
Mlle	Mademoiselle
MV	Motor vessel
No (Nos)	number(s)
pm	post meridiem, after noon
PS (PS)	postscript
PPS (PPS)	a second postscript
RSVP	Réspondez s il vous plait (please reply)
Sen	Senior
S/S (SS)	Steamship

The following should be typed in full unless appearing in accounts:

a/c	account
b/d	brought down

Task 90

Typist: One copy, please. If there 2 pages for photocopying display so that charts are complete on any one page (no take over)

BUSINESS DATA ILLUSTRATED

as an example, the sales of 2 departments in a company will be taken:

Department X	Cash sales	£6,000	Total sales £22,000
	Credit sales	£4,000	
	H.P. sales	£12,000	
Department Y	Cash sales	£8,000	Total sales £26,000
	Credit sales	£12,000	
	H.P. sales	£6,000	

a) BAR CHART

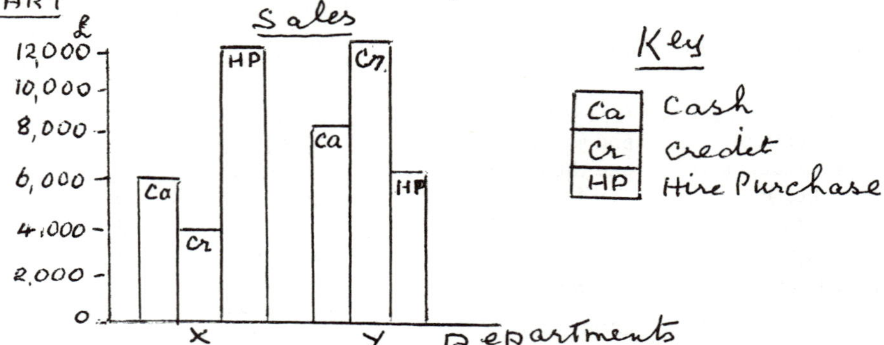

Each item is shaded, coloured, or shown in a different way, & a key is given. A space usually separates one set of data fr. another.

b) COMPONENT BAR CHART

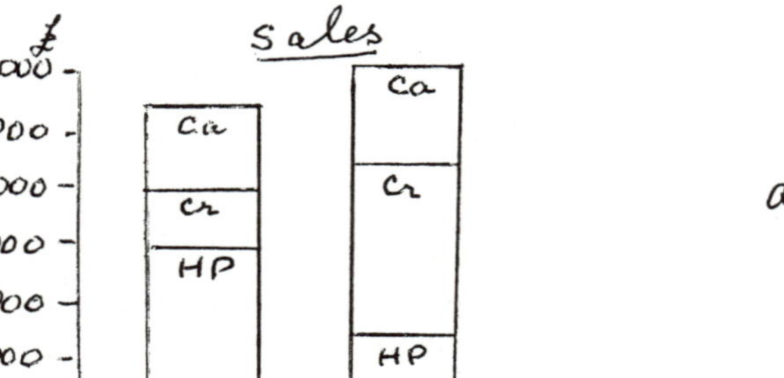

Key

as above

This is used to represent an overall total, each Bar being made up of the individual items in each set, built up one upon the other.

B/E	Bill of exchange
b/f	brought forward
B/L	Bill of lading
B.S.	Balance sheet, bill of sale
c/d	carried down
c/f	carried forward
cifc & i	Cost, insurance, freight, commission and interest
C/N	Credit note
Cr	credit, creditor
cum div	with dividend
CWO	Cash with order
Do	Ditto
Dr	debit, debtor
Ex lib	Ex libris (from the library of)
fas	free alongside ship
fob	free on board
for	free on rail
HP	horse power, hire purchase
inst	instant, this month
Inc	Incorporated
pa	per annum
P/A	Power of Attorney
PA	personal assistant
prox	proximo, next month
R/D	Refer to drawer (Banking)
ult	ultimo, last month

Abbreviations always typed without the full stop. There are certain categories of words which do not take a full stop after the abbreviation:

a symbols: @ £ & %;
b 1st, 2nd, 3rd, 4th, etc;
c re, per, pro forma, per cent, etc;
d abbreviations separated by the solidus: a/c, B/L, etc;
e metric units: 6 cm, 200 m, etc.

Abbreviations in general use (with or without full stops)

A.A.	Automobile Association
A.D.C.	Aide-de-Camp
A.E.A.	Atomic Energy Authority
A.P.	Associated Press
A.S.R.	Air-Sea Rescue
B.A.	British Airways
B.B.C.	British Broadcasting Corporation
B.I.R.	Board of Inland Revenue
B.M.A.	British Medical Association
B.M.J.	British Medical Journal
B.R.	British Rail
B.R.C.	British Red Cross
B.S.I.	British Standards Institution
C.B.I.	Confederation of British Industries
C.C.	County Council
C.I.D.	Criminal Investigation Department
C.N.D.	Campaign for Nuclear Disarmament
D.E.	Department of Employment
D.H.S.S.	Department of Health and Social Security
D.o.E.	Department of the Environment
E.E.C.	European Economic Community
E.F.T.A. (Efta)	European Free Trade Association
ERNIE	Electronic Random Numbers Indicator Equipment
E.S.A.	European Space Agency
G.A.T.T. (Gatt)	General Agreement on Tariffs and Trade
G.M.T.	Greenwich Mean/Meridian Time
G.M.C.	General Medical Council
H.M.S.O.	Her/His Majesty's Stationery Office
I.B.A.	Independent Broadcasting Authority
I.C.I.	Imperial Chemical Industries
I.S.O.	International Standards Organisation
J.P.	Justice of the Peace
M.A.F.F.	Ministry of Agriculture, Fisheries and Food
M.O.H.	Medical Officer of Health
M.P.	Member of Parliament
M.R.C.	Medical Research Council
N.A.L.G.O. (Nalgo)	National and Local Government Officers' Association
N.A.T.O. (Nato)	North Atlantic Treaty Organisation
N.F.U.	National Farmers' Union
N.H.S.	National Health Service
N.R.D.C.	National Research Development Corporation
O.D.A.	Overseas Development Administration
O.E.C.D.	Organization for Economic Co-operation and Development
O.H.M.S.	On Her/His Majesty's Service
O. & M.	Organisation and Methods
P.C.	Privy Council(lor); Police Constable
P.A.Y.E.	Pay as you earn
P.E.R.T.	Programme Evaluation and Review Technique
P.L.A.	Port of London Authority
P.M.	Prime Minister
P.M.G.	Postmaster-General
Q.C.	Queen's Counsel

Task 88

Typist Please type the Financial Review & head up for the last 5 years – this year first.

a) FIVE-YEAR FINANCIAL REVIEW

	(TY) 19-- £000	(LY) 19-- £000	19-- £000	19-- £000	19-- £000
Sales	452,225	401,255	324,192	273,569	244,326
Profit before taxation	39,658	41,829	33,578	27,022	25,498
Taxation	12,052	11,068	10,969	12,395	9,256
Profit after tax	27,606	30,761	22,609	14,627	16,242
Extraordinary items	-	591	241	147	250
Preference dividends	20	20	20	21	21
Ordinary dividends	9,228	8,955	7,154	6,405	5,734
Retained profit	18,358	21,195	15,194	8,054	10,237
Shareholders' interests	150,331	132,179	109,484	93,622	85,287
Deferred tax	1,754	1,957	518	211	-
Loans	29,802	4,382	4,656	4,827	5,013
Capital employed	181,887	138,518	114,658	98,660	90,300
Fixed assets & investments	140,828	121,336	93,218	78,217	66,740
Deferred asset	-	-	786	1,710	1,614
Net current assets	41,059	17,182	20,654	18,733	21,946
Employment of capital	181,887	138,518	114,658	98,660	90,300

Task 89

Set out the Sales figures on A5
Send these figures as a memo to Mr. F. Jones, Market Research for information & interest (from A. McDonald, Chief Accountant)

SALES	(TY) 19-- £000	(LY) 19-- £000	Increase %
Merchandise in Store	350,653	314,932	+ 11.3
Food	74,929	63,460	+ 18.1
Restaurant	26,643	22,863	+ 16.5
	£452,225	£401,255	+ 12.7

R.A.C.	Royal Automobile Club
R.A.D.A.	Royal Academy of Dramatic Art
R.D.C.	Rural District Council
S.E.A.T.O. (Seato)	South East-Asia Treaty Organisation
S.P.C.K.	Society for Promoting Christian Knowledge
S.R.N.	State Registered Nurse
S.T.D.	Subscriber Trunk Dialling
T.U.C.	Trades Union Congress
T.G.W.U.	Transport and General Workers' Union
U.D.C.	Urban District Council
U.N.	United Nations
U.N.E.S.C.O. (Unesco)	United Nations Educational, Scientific and Cultural Organisation
U.N.I.C.E.F. (Unicef)	United Nations International Children's Emergency Fund
U.N.R.R.A.	United Nations Relief and Rehabilitation Administration
W.E.A.	Workers' Educational Association
W.H.O.	World Health Organisation
W.R.V.S.	Women's Royal Voluntary Service
Y.H.A.	Youth Hostels Association
Y.M.C.A.	Young Men's Christian Association
Y.W.C.A.	Young Women's Christian Association

Order for decorations

V.C.	Victoria Cross
G.C.	George Cross
K.G.	Knight of the Most Noble Order of the Garter
K.T.	Knight of the Most Ancient and Most Noble Order of the Thistle
K.P.	Knight of the Most Illustrious Order of St. Patrick
P.C.	Privy Councillor
G.C.B.	Knight Grand Cross of the Most Honourable Order of the Bath
O.M.	Order of Merit
G.C.S.I.	Knight Grand Commander of the Most Exalted Order of the Star of India
G.C.M.G.	Knight Grand Cross of the Most Distinguished Order of St. Michael and St. George
G.C.M.G.	Dame Grand Cross of the Most Distinguished Order of St. Michael and St. George
G.C.I.E.	Knight Grand Commander of the Most Eminent Order of the Indian Empire
V.A.	Royal Order of Victoria and Albert
C.I.	Imperial Order of the Crown of India
G.C.V.O.	Knight Grand Cross of the Royal Victorian Order
D.C.V.O.	Dame Grand Cross of the Royal Victorian Order
G.B.E.	Knight Grand Cross of the Most Excellent Order of the British Empire
G.B.E.	Dame Grand Cross of the Most Excellent Order of the British Empire
C.H.	Companion of Honour
K.C.B.	Knight Commander of the Most Honourable Order of the Bath
K.C.S.I.	Knight Commander of the Most Exalted Order of the Star of India
K.C.M.G.	Knight Commander of the Most Distinguished Order of St. Michael and St. George
K.C.I.E.	Knight Commander of the Most Eminent Order of the Indian Empire
K.C.V.O.	Knight Commander of the Royal Victorian Order
K.B.E.	Knight Commander of the Most Excellent Order of the British Empire
D.B.E.	Dame Commander of the Most Excellent Order of the British Empire
C.B.	Companion of the Most Honourable Order of the Bath
C.S.I.	Companion of the Most Exalted Order of the Star of India
C.M.G.	Companion of the Most Distinguished Order of St. Michael and St. George
C.I.E.	Companion of the Most Eminent Order of the Indian Empire
C.V.O.	Commander of the Royal Victorian Order
C.B.E.	Commander of the Most Excellent Order of the British Empire
D.S.O.	Distinguished Service Order
M.V.O.	Member of the Royal Victorian Order (4th class)
O.B.E.	Office of the Most Excellent Order of the British Empire

Task 86

KNIGHT STARR LTD – SUBSIDIARY COMPANY – BALANCE SHEET at 1st April 19..

		(TY) 19..		(LY) 19..
Capital Employed	£000	£000	£000	£000
Share capital		20		20
Retained profit		32		61
		52		81
Use of Capital				
Fixed assets		9,382		9,664
Current assets				
Debtors	240		109	
c/c Cash at Bank + short-term deposit	1,537		840	
	1,777		949	
Current liabilities				
Creditors + provisions	1401		445	
Taxation	357		–	7/
Short-term loan + bank overdraft	531		406	
	2289		851	
c/c Net Current (liabilities)/assets		(512)		98
		8870		9762
Deduct				
Deferred taxation	4877		5023	
Regional development grants	35		43	
Long- + medium-term liabilities	3906		4615	
		8818		9681
		52		81

Task 87

Memo, please, to Mr. J. Waring, Gen. Man. (from Mr. H. Tubb, A/cs) Enclose this "Note 20" from the B/S as requested. Will arrange with Sec. convenient time to discuss matter within next few days.

EXPIRATION OF LEASES (NOTE 20)

	TY 19.. Land + buildings £m	Other £m	Total £m	LY 19.. Land + buildings £m	Other £m	Total £m
Within one year	1.0	1.0	2.0	0.7	0.4	1.1
From 2 to 5 yrs.	3.4	3.1	6.5	2.7	2.1	4.8
Over 5 yrs.	20.9	0.2	21.1	18.1	0.4	18.5
	25.3	4.3	29.6	21.5	2.9	24.3

M.V.O.	Member of the Royal Victorian Order (5th class)	C.G.M.	Conspicuous Gallantry Medal
M.B.E.	Member of the Most Excellent Order of the British Empire	G.M.	George Medal
R.R.C.	Royal Red Cross	D.S.M.	Distinguished Service Medal
D.S.C.	Distinguished Service Cross	M.M.	Military Medal
M.C.	Military Cross	D.F.M.	Distinguished Flying Medal
D.F.C.	Distinguished Flying Cross	A.F.M.	Air Force Medal
A.F.C.	Air Force Cross	S.G.M.	Sea Gallantry Medal
A.R.R.C.	Associate, Royal Red Cross	Q.G.M.	Queen's Gallantry Medal
A.M.	Albert Medal	B.E.M.	British Empire Medal
D.C.M.	Distinguished Conduct Medal	T.D.	Territorial Decoration
		E.D.	Efficiency Decoration

Fellow of the

F.C.A.	Institute of Chartered Accountants in England and Wales	F.R.C.M.	Royal College of Music
F.C.C.A.	Association of Certified Accountants	F.R.C.P.	Royal College of Physicians
F.C.I.I.	Chartered Insurance Institute	F.R.C.S.	Royal College of Surgeons
F.C.I.S.	Institute of Chartered Secretaries and Administrators	F.R.C.V.S.	Royal College of Veterinary Surgeons
F.C.M.A.	Institute of Cost and Management Accountants	F.R.G.S.	Royal Geographical Society
F.F.A.	Faculty of Actuaries	F.R.H.S.	Royal Horticultural Society
F.G.S.	Geological Society	F.R.I.B.A.	Royal Institute of British Architects
F.I.A.	Institute of Actuaries	F.R.I.C.S.	Royal Institution of Chartered Surveyors
F.R.C.S.	Royal Society of Chemistry	F.R.S.	Royal Society
F.J.I.	Institute of Journalists	F.R.S.A.	Royal Society of Arts
F.R.A.S.	Royal Astronomical Society	F.R.S.L.	Royal Society of Literature
		F.Z.S.	Zoological Society

Member of the

M.I.C.E.	Institution of Civil Engineers	M.R.C.P.	Royal College of Physicians
M.I.E.E.	Institution of Electrical Engineers	M.R.C.S.	Royal College of Surgeons
M.I.Mech.E.	Institution of Mechanical Engineers	M.R.C.V.S.	Royal College of Veterinary Surgeons
M.P.S.	Pharmaceutical Society		

Associate Member of the

A.M.I.C.E.	Institution of Civil Engineers	A.M.I.Mech.E.	Institution of Mechanical Engineers
A.M.I.Chem.E.	Institution of Chemical Engineers		
A.M.I.E.E.	Institution of Electrical Engineers		

Associate of the

A.C.A.	Institute of Chartered Accountants	A.R.A.	Royal Academy
A.C.I.I.	Chartered Insurance Institute	A.R.A.M.	Royal Academy of Music
A.C.I.S.	Chartered Institute of Secretaries and Administrators	A.R.I.B.A.	Royal Institute of British Architects
A.C.W.A.	Institute of Cost and Works Accountants	A.R.I.C.S.	Royal Institution of Chartered Surveyors
A.I.A.	Institute of Actuaries		

THE ALPHA BUILDING SOCIETY

Balance Sheet as at 30th September 19—*

	19—*	19—‡		19—*	19—‡
	£'000	£'000		£,000	£,000
Due to Investing Shareholders	4,500	4,222	Balances due or outstanding on mortgages	4,062	3,840
Deposits and loans (net from Bank)	67	62	Investments:		
Taxation and other liabilities:			Listed (Market Value £390,000 19—I £410,000)	385	405
Corporation tax	12	9	Unquoted	190	100
Income tax	7	5	Interest accrued	3	3
Sundry Creditors	4	3			
	23	17		578	508
Deferred taxation	8	6	Cash at bank and in hand	64	60
General reserve	154	149	Debtors	1	2
			Office Premises (Freehold at cost less depreciation)	28	29
			Office Equipment (at cost less depreciation)	16	15
			Other assets	3	2
	£4,752	£4,456		£4,752	£4,456

Report of the Auditors to the Members of
The Alpha Building Society

We have audited the annexed financial statements in accordance with approved Auditing Standards.

In our view the financial statements which have been prepared under the historical cost convention give, under that convention, a true and fair view of the state of the Society's affairs at 31st September 19—* and of its income and expenditure and movement of funds for the year then ended and are drawn up in accordance with the Building Societies Act 1962 and the regulations made thereunder.

15 November 19—*
LONDON

ANDREW BURRELL
Chartered Accountants

* This year
‡ Last year

Other qualifications

L.D.S.	Licentiate in Dental Surgery
L.R.A.M.	Licentiate of the Royal Academy of Music
L.R.C.P.	Licentiate of the Royal College of Physicians
L.S.A.	Licentiate of the Society of Apothecaries
B.A.	Bachelor of Arts
B.C.L.	Bachelor of Civil Law
B.Com.	Bachelor of Commerce
B.D.	Bachelor of Divinity
B.Sc.	Bachelor of Science
D.C.L.	Doctor of Civil Law
D.Phil	Doctor of Philosophy
D.Sc.	Doctor of Science
LL.B.	Bachelor of Laws
LL.D	Doctor of Laws
M.A.	Master of Arts
M.B.	Bachelor of Medicine
M.Com.	Master of Commerce
M.D.	Doctor of Medicine
Mus.B. or Mus. Bac.	Bachelor of Music
Mus. D. or Mus.Doc.	Doctor of Music
Ph.D.	Doctor of Philosophy

Foreign words and phrases in common use

ab initio	from the beginning
ad hoc	for one special purpose (*see* page 133)
ad infinitum	to infinity; indefinitely
ad valorem	(abbr. ad val.), according to the value
al fresco	in the open air
amour propre	vanity; self-esteem
anno domini	in the year of our Lord
au fait	expert; well instructed in
bête noire	pet aversion
bona fide	in good faith
carte blanche	full discretionary powers, free to act
chef d'oeuvre	a masterpiece
circa	about
compos mentis	of sane mind
compte rendu	an account rendered, a report
cordon bleu	(lit. blue ribbon), a first-class cook, a culinary method
coup d'état	a political sudden exercise of force
de facto	in actual fact
de jure	by right
de rigueur	required by custom
de trop	too much, superfluous
en bloc	together, in the mass
erratum	(pl. errata), error, mistake in printing or writing
et seq	and the following
extra vires	outside one's powers
fait accompli	an accomplished fact, something already done
faux pas	a false step, a blunder
in camera	privately, not in open court
infra	below
infra dig	undignified
in loco parentis	in the place of a parent
in situ	in position
inter alia	among other things
interim	in the meantime
intra vires	within one's powers
ipso facto	by the fact itself, automatically
multum in parvo	much in little
pari passu	in equal proportion
per capita	by heads, the number of people
prima facie	at first sight
pro et con	for and against
pro rata	in proportion
pro tem.	for the time being
quid pro quo	one thing for another; compensation for a service
résumé	a summary
savoir faire	knowledge of the world; tact
sine qua non	an indispensable condition
status quo	as things stand or stood
sub judice	still under consideration by the courts
sub poena	under a penalty, a writ to secure a person's appearance in court
supra	above, formerly
tête-à-tête	face to face; a private conversation
ultra vires	beyond the powers or rights possessed
verbatim	word for word
vice versa	the order being reversed

Bar and pie charts

In the same way that organisation charts provide a quick ‘picture’ of the structure of an organisation, so bar and pie charts, used extensively in offices in one form or another, give an immediate visual comparison of various facets of a business – from finances to stationery and disposition of staff. They are simple to produce, but care is needed in their execution.

Bar charts. For these (as for line graphs) there are two elements in the statistics: a left-hand vertical line joined at right angles by a base horizontal line. Measured marks along both lines, beginning at the joining point, indicate increasing factors, or other specific data. Shading or colouring is frequently used to differentiate between the items concerned, when a ‘key’ must be provided.

Pie charts. These indicate, by means of a circle (360°), the proportion of the whole occupied by individual components. Explanations can be given by shading, colouring, or wording typed within the segments. A compass, protractor and ruler are recommended for completion of this type of work.

Task 83

To: W. B. Tredwell & Co. 189 West Road, Manchester, M16 8RV
From: Fairbanks & Luckie, 77 Grove Road, Manchester, M16 7RW

9 yards Stair Carpeting, 22″ @ £2.50
12 ″ ″ ″ 36″ @ £3.00
7 ″ ″ ″ Saxony 27″ @ £2.30
2 Axminster Carpets – 10′ 6″ x 10′ 6″ @ £200
1 Turkey Carpet, No. 86, 11′ 4″ x 8′ 4″ @ £150
1 ″ ″ No. 90, 12′ 9″ x 9′ 10″ @ £170
2 Tea Sets ‘Devonia’, 21 pieces @ £45
4 ″ ″ ‘Countess’, 42 pieces @ £120
2 Dinner Services ‘Ella’ 25 pieces @ £140
4 Fruit Service ‘Pearman’ 13 pieces @ £45
1 Lamp stand, standard base – £26
2 ‘Heatwell’ convector heaters @ £35
3 Wooden coffee tables @ £25
6 Wooden trays (cut-out handles) @ £7

Total (to be calculated)

INVOICE

194

FAIRBANKS & LUCKIE
77 Grove Road
MANCHESTER
M16 7RW

Date

Terms: Net Cash

STATEMENT

A J COUCH LIMITED

Orchard Road
HIGH WYCOMBE
Bucks

Date

Date	Details	Debit	Credit	Balance

Task 84

STATEMENT
To: The Ultra Furniture Stores Ltd, Commercial Road, Portsmouth, PO1 1BA
From: A.J. Couch Limited, Orchard Road, High Wycombe, Bucks.

July 1 – To account rendered – £13.05
July 2 – Invoice 77 – £105.50
July 6 – Invoice 80 – £35.75
July 12 – Invoice 90 – £215.25
July 17 – Invoice 112 – £11.50
July 22 – Invoice 123 – £75.60
July 24 – By cheque £456.65
July 29 – Invoice 148 – £243.00
Balance (to be calculated)
E. & O.E.

6 Correspondence and Communications (General Theory)

Letters are the 'shop window' of a business and can do much to make or mar its prestige, especially in the introductory period when contact is made with new clients. Great care must be taken in the general appearance of all typed communications.

It is the responsibility of the firm or organization to provide headed notepaper of a good quality, but it is the typist who is responsible for ensuring that the letter ready for signature is attractive and artistic in general display, as well as being clean and crisp in appearance, and of course, accurate in content.

Letters are, perhaps, more attractive when they are placed centrally on the page with even margins (varying according to the length of the letter)—but many offices today have their own individual styles of display, and the typist must be prepared to follow the 'Rules of the House' when necessary. Whatever the display, however, the typist should produce a letter of a high standard of which she is proud.

Typing is a skill and an art, and the craftsman, in every field, should be proud of his/her creation.

It is suggested that students should read through the information given to refresh their memories on the many points concerned with letters, before typing the correspondence which follows.

General Letters (Traditional Indented Style)

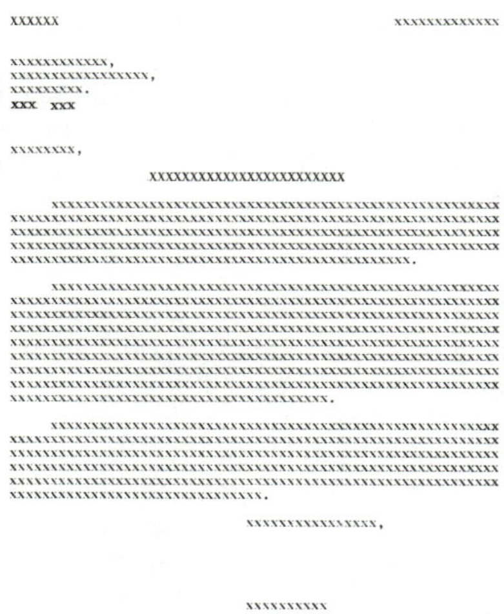

Date Always type day before month (to prevent possible confusion of figures), eg 1*st July*, 19-- (with or without punctuation), also 1 *July*, 19--. (The American style is to type day after month).

Reference Usually typed in line with the date unless a space is indicated in the printed heading. The initials of the dictator are typed first, then those of the typist (sometimes the typist's initials are in lower case!), followed by the subject or file reference.

Inside address Keep to three or four lines if possible, bringing the county on to the line with the town if necessary. Always use single spacing in either blocked or indented style, at the top or foot of the page. Never abbreviate Street, Road, Avenue, etc. Lines should end with a comma, except the last which should be the postcode, with *no* punctuation, usually on a separate line.

Salutation Always typed up to the left-hand margin and two spaces above the body of the letter.

Subject heading Typed two spaces down from the salutation, centred over the letter, and usually underscored. Never followed with a full stop unless the heading ends with a recognized abbreviation.

Side headings When a letter deals with several subjects, use either shoulder or paragraph headings.

a The shoulder heading begins at the margin and occupies a separate line. It is either in lower case and underscored or in capitals. The information follows as an ordinary indented paragraph two line spaces below.

b The paragraph heading begins at the paragraph indentation, is usually in capitals, followed by a full stop or dash (with appropriate spacing for the punctuation used), and the information runs on as an ordinary paragraph.

Insets A passage separated from the main part of the letter has two line spaces before the first paragraph and two after the last paragraph, and is

11 Accounts and Financial Statements

Although the computer, accounting machine and other sophisticated equipment are responsible for the quick and accurate production of most accounts, the typist is still required to prepare documents for many different purposes, and must be sufficiently well trained to be able to undertake *any* of them. In the smaller firms, of course, she is still 'Jack of all trades – and master of *all*'!

Whilst it is desirable to have some knowledge of accounts it is not essential, so long as there is an *understanding* of the basic and underlying principles, ie the reason for the Trading Account, Profit and Loss Account, Balance Sheet and Reviews. It is important to appreciate the *purpose* of the financial statement so as to present it in a clear style enabling the reader to interpret it and extract the specific information required – often to prepare other and varied statements for analysis and comparisons of figures.

Typing techniques

Requirements for the typing of accounts are:

1 Accuracy and an ability to check one's work correctly (preferably with another person).
2 Correct alignment of figures (units under units, tens under tens, etc.).
3 Consistency in the use/non-use of commas in thousands, millions, etc.
4 Correct positioning of the currency symbol.
5 Ability to 'box in' information, and type neat double lines for totals.

All financial statements should be *centred* on the page (or over two pages if joining is necessary), with *all figures absolutely clear*, doubtful figures or display having been verified with the originator. '*Loss*' amounts should be shown in a consistent manner, usually by underscoring or 'boxing in'.

Offices generally have their own 'House Styles' which will be fully explained before a typist is asked to produce specific work of any complexity. Common sense, adaptability, good typing techniques and expertise in following 'copy' are essential for this branch of work.

Balance sheets

Horizontal. Where balance sheets and other accounts are typed horizontally, side by side, the totals of both sides must align. (The shorter side is typed first, omitting the total, which will be typed at the same time as, and level with, that of the longer side). The double lines under both totals will be typed in the same manner. Comparative figures for a previous period are often given in a separate column, and are usually given in a different colour when printed.

Two-page Accounts. In an accountant's office typewriters with extra long carriages are provided to take the special large paper required for producing accounts of all descriptions. However, if two sheets of A4 are to be used, first the longer side is typed – complete – then the shorter, pencil marks having indicated the position for beginning the centred heading, the starting and finishing points and the total lines, to ensure correct alignment when the sheets are joined on the back with transparent tape.

Vertical. In the vertical layout, the Assets are usually typed first, and may be described as 'Assets Employed' (or 'Use of Capital'), and the Liabilities follow below, with the words 'Financed by' (or 'Capital Employed'). The order and terms may, however, vary.

Invoices

Invoices may be displayed in many different ways, so common sense must be used in their completion.

For a one-day order, the date of purchase is typed in the upper section, and the items purchased in the wide details column; price per item is typed in the narrow column on the right, or the '@' sign is used after the item, followed by the price per article, metre, etc. (The '@' sign is also used to show price per item when typing quotations.)

For invoices sent out at the end of the month, the date of typing is shown in the upper section, and the dates when the purchases were made are inserted in the narrow left-hand margin.

Statements

These are usually sent out monthly, and enumerate only the numbers of the invoices and the amounts owing.

indented equally from both margins in order to be centred. Where possible the left-hand margin should begin at a point to the right of the main paragraph indent. The paragraphs should be either in hanging or blocked style (see below), and in single spacing. If items or paragraphs are numbered, small roman numerals i, ii, or small letters *a, b* are used, leaving two spaces after the bracket before beginning the paragraph.

Paragraphs Those used in the main body of the letter are 'indented', those used in inset passages are either 'hanging' or 'block' paragraphs.

a **Indented paragraphs** The first word of the paragraph begins at a predetermined number of spaces to the right of the main margin. This indent is usually half an inch or one inch. Always use double spacing between paragraphs.

b **Hanging paragraphs** The second and subsequent lines begin two or three spaces to the right of the first word in the paragraph. Double spacing between paragraphs is more attractive, but single is permissible, especially in one-line, numbered (or lettered) items.

c **Block or flush paragraphs** Each line begins at the same point of the scale. *Always* use double spacing between paragraphs.

Subscription (or Complimentary Close) This is typed two line spaces down from the last line of the letter, beginning at the centre of the page, the initial letter of the *first* word only being typed in capitals.

When the name of the company is included, this is centred under the subscription, one space down if the letter is in single spacing, two spaces down if in double spacing, and it is usually in capitals.

Designation Typed five or six spaces below the subscription, to leave space for the signature, in line with the first letter of the subscription, or centred under it.

It is usual to type the name of the signatory below the actual signature (which may be illegible). It is either centred immediately above the designation or blocked, according to the style of display.

Enclosures Typed in full or as an abbreviation at the bottom left-hand margin. If there is more than one enclosure, the number should be stated.

Continuation sheets The second and subsequent pages of a business letter (followers) are always typed on plain paper and should contain the following information:

a Name of the addressee (at the left-hand margin with no final punctuation, unless ending with the abbreviation Esq.).

b Page number (centred).
c Date (to end at the right-hand margin).

Messrs. Black & White - 2 - *1st July*, 19--

These particulars are typed on one line, about one inch from the top of the paper. Should these be cramped, the name and date are typed two spaces below the page number. When a continuation page is used, there must be at least three lines of type in addition to the complimentary close.

Postscript This is not always an afterthought, but is often deliberately added at the end of a letter to draw attention to a particular point.

P.S. or PS. is typed about an inch below the designation, and up to the left-hand margin. The message stands out clearly if it is typed as an inset, in single spacing, usually as a block paragraph and indented half an inch from the right margin. Usually the signatory initials a postscript.

Private, Confidential, etc To ensure the privacy of a letter, the words giving the instruction are typed either in capitals or lower case and underscored, two spaces above the inside address on the letter and above the addressee's name on the envelope.

Personal A personal letter sent to business premises may have the inside address typed at the foot of the page. The word '*Personal*' is typed two spaces above the salutation, in which the christian name is often used, and is handwritten for courtesy by the sender when signing the letter. '*Personal*' must also appear on the envelope.

'Attention' line Some business houses require that 'all correspondence be addressed to the company and not to individuals'. However, to ensure that the person dealing with a particular matter shall receive the letter, an 'attention' line is added (also on the envelope).

The following points should be noted:

a The Attention line is inserted two spaces below the inside address.
b The salutation refers to the Company, not to the person named in the Attention line, eg:

Messrs. Allen & Wicks,
Braintree Works,
Birmingham B14 9AW
B14 9AW

For the attention of Miss Edwards

Dear Sirs,

The attention line could also read:

Attention of Miss Edwards or
Attention: Miss Edwards

Task 82

Typist Please type this programme, as a folded booklet, for the Bornchurch Ensemble. They are giving a Popular Concert at the Seaforth Hall, Bornchurch, on the last Saturday of next month at 8 p.m. Display attractively. On P. 4 give an acknowledgement to the Warden and Management Committee for the use of the hall.

Artists: Netty Mayo (soprano) Ross Flemming (tenor)
David Williams (Baritone) Martyn Webster (violin)
Conductor Walter Kale

PROGRAMME

1. Viennese Waltzes — Johann Strauss
3 ~~2~~. Selection: The Desert Song — Romberg
4 ~~3~~. Violin Solos:
Allegro — Fiocco
Mazurka — Wieniawski
u.c. 5 ~~4~~. Selection: Perchance to dream — Ivor Novello
2 ~~5~~. Songs:
The Open Road — Nigel Brooks
Drake goes West — Wilfrid Sanderson

INTERVAL

6. Ballads of Britain — arr. Byfield
8 ~~7~~. Selection: Lilac Time — Schubert
7 ~~8~~. Songs:
l.c. The Green hills o'Somerset — Eric Coates
Waiting for you — Leslie James
9. Violin Solo:
If my songs were only winged — Reynaldo Hahn
10. Song: Velia (The Merry Widow) — Franz Lehar
11. Selection: The Nutcracker Suite — Tchaikofsky

FIN

Note Please add the following right across the 2 inside pages - in caps.

Light refreshments will be served during the interval

Fully-blocked Style Letter

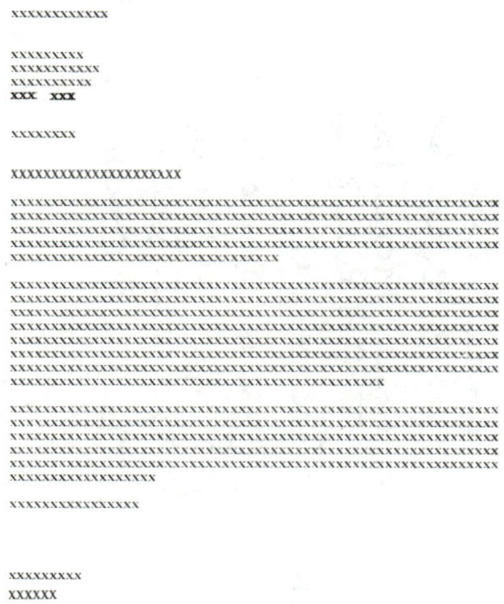

For various reasons, the paramount one being that of speed, many firms use the fully blocked style of letters. This requires that *everything* is typed at the margin.

Details on the continuation sheet are all typed up to the left-hand margin, page number, addressee, and date.

Semi-blocked Style Letter

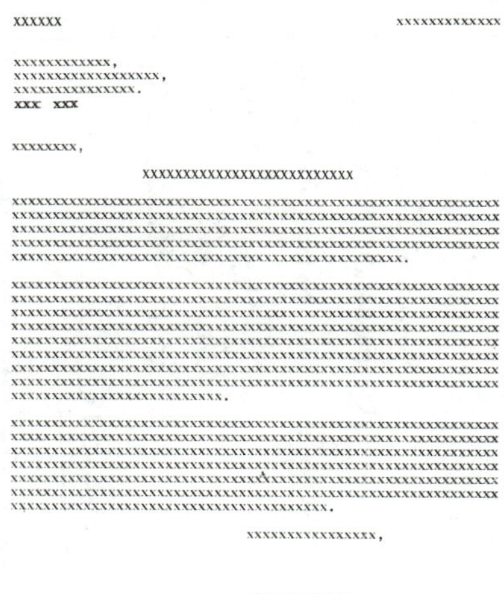

This is similar to the fully-blocked style, except that the date, subject heading, subscription and designation are not typed at the left-hand margin, but are indented as in the traditional letter.

Punctuation

Open punctuation is normally used in the typing of the date, inside address, salutation and complimentary close of blocked and semi-blocked letters. Full stops are also omitted following abbreviations.

At all times normal punctuation is used in the body of the letter and consistency should be maintained when typing dates, etc.

Circular letters

Current practice is often to reproduce these letters to look like individually typed personal letters, with or without the inside address, and sometimes using the addressee's name in the salutation and in various other parts of the letter. Word processors and other machines enable firms to personalise all communications of a general nature. However, without such machines, the typist needs to make the following modifications to normal letters:

a Name and address of the firm sending the letter is either printed, or typed by the typist.
b Date is often given as: '*Date as postmark*' or month and year only.
c Probably there is no reference.
d Salutation: *Dear Madam,* or *Dear Sir*, or *Dear Sir or Madam.*
e The signature is included on the master copy.

Letters to several people

These can be divided into two categories—outgoing, and internal.

a **Outgoing** It may occasionally be necessary to send an identical letter to three or four people, all of whom are to receive a top copy.

A carbon copy is taken of the first letter only, and the names and addresses, in alphabetical order and in single spacing are added to the top of that carbon copy afterwards. For clarity, the added information is typed on one line for each addressee, and, if all are in the same area, the town need not be included. A tick on the left-hand side of the name is added as each letter is completed.

b **Internal** If copies of a typed letter have to be sent to several people within the firm for information or action, the requisite number of carbon copies is taken in addition to the file copy unless photocopies can be taken of the original.

i Each carbon copy is clearly headed, usually at the top, with the name of the person and/or department to whom it is to be sent underscored. The name may be preceded by *For the attention of* . . . or *Attention of* . . . or *Information of* . . . (This depends on the Rules of the House.)

ii File copy is headed *copies to* . . . or *cc* . . . and the names are typed down the page in single spacing in alphabetical order.

If needed that everybody shall know who has seen the communication, the information is typed on the top copy and on the carbons.

Pages 4 & 5

FOLLIES OF THE WEST

PART I

1. The Debut
Harry Jacobs
Glyn Williams
Percy Pullen Ensemble

2. Sunrise – The Debutantes
Mary Maughan
Barbara Finch, Johanah Stuart
Jack Benford

3. The Pace Makers
Herbert Griggs & his Trio

4. Storm in a Teacup
Mary Maughan
Henry Jacobs
P.P. Ensemble

5. The Midgets
Susie Petit
Flora Short
John Trenwell, Tiny Small

6. Piccadilly
P.P. Ensemble

7. The Rendez-vous
Patrick O'Neil
Llewellyn Jones
Sandy McTavish

8. The Shadows
Florence Grey
David Johnson
Doreen's Dancers

9. The Sound of Music
Mary Maughan
Glyn Williams
Llewellyn Jones
P.P. Ensemble.

INTERVAL

PART II

10. The Picture Gallery
Barbara Finch
Susie Petit
Patrick O'Neil
Henry Jacobs.

11. Down Under
John Deighton
Tiny Small
P.P. Ensemble.

12. Rhapsody in Blue
David Johnson
Tiny Small
Mary Maughan
Doreen's Dancers

13. Noonday Sun
Glyn Williams
Henry Jacobs
Sandy McTavish

14. Thou and Me – or Two's Company
John Trenwell
Henry Jacobs
Barbara Finch

15. Flowerland
Doreen's Dancers
P. P Ensemble

16. The Cascade – – –
Mary Maughan
Jack Benford

17. Sunset
Herbert Griggs & his Trio
– – – Henry Jacobs
Glyn Williams

18. Home to Roost – Finale
Doreen's Dancers
The Full Company.

FIN

Typist (Each artist on a separate line please & justify R.H. margins)

iii File copy names should be ticked on the left when the letters have been sent.

iv To facilitate quick recognition of copies sent to particular people or departments, tinted flimsy paper, or coloured carbon paper may be used.

Copy of a letter

Most offices today have photocopiers, so that if a copy of an incoming letter were required, it would be speedily reproduced by this means, which has the added advantage of including the actual signature (and any possible error).

If such a machine were unobtainable, the following points should be noted:

a The word *Copy* in capitals (or underscored) should be typed at the top left-hand corner.
b As much of the printed heading as is relevant should be given, ie name, type of firm, address, etc.
c Everything which appears in type *must* be copied.
d The text should be copied exactly. If there is a mistake, this should be included, with the addition of (*sic*) after it, to indicate that the error appeared in the original and was not made by the typist copying the letter.
e After the subscription, three spaces down and to the left of it the word (*Signed*) should be typed in brackets, followed by the name of the signatory, typed in full capitals, exactly as the signature appears on the letter being copied; and three spaces further down the designation if there is one.

Draft of a letter

If a letter is required in draft form, the word *Draft* should always appear in the top left-hand corner.

The letter may be typed exactly as it is to appear in its final form, or it may be in double or treble spacing with wide margins if it is to undergo extensive revision. The typist must be sure she understands the instruction before beginning the letter.

Form letters

These are printed or duplicated letters used by firms in reply to enquiries which do not require individual letters. The typist has only to insert the necessary details. Great care is needed in matching up, or obtaining the correct alignment.

Specimen letters

This refers to a series of letters (each allotted a different number or letter) which are used as 'skeletons' or specimens by the typist when stock answers are required. They are often used in accounts departments when reminding customers of their overdue accounts. Unlike form letters, these are typed as ordinary, individual letters, with the given information added in the appropriate places

Formal reply to an invitation

If an invitation is printed and formal, the reply should always be in the third person and the wording of the invitation should be copied. If accepting, the occasion, place, date and time should be given: if refusing, the occasion, place and date only need be mentioned, and the reason for refusing (prior engagement!).

Note the following general points:

a Type on card or A5 paper.
b Address at top (displayed attractively).
c Body centred, with equal margins and no division at line ends.
d Double-line spacing.
e Date often at the foot, at left-hand margin.
f Envelope addressed to wife (or hostess)

Air mail letters

Air Mail letters can be purchased from the Post Office for use outside Europe. Specially thin paper may be used if several pages are required, or if enclosures are necessary. A blue 'Air Mail' label is required if it is not already printed on the envelope which is also of specially thin quality. A lighter touch is required on this thin paper.

Professional correspondence

A5 paper and elite typewriter pitch are generally used by private secretaries in the offices of professional men. The inside address is sometimes typed at the *end* of their letters. Enclosures are usually indicated *after* the inside address though they *may* appear before it. Continuation sheets contain only the page number. The secretary would naturally have to be prepared to adopt whichever style her employer prefers.

The above points may, of course, apply to the purely commercial letter if the executive so wishes – but usually the inside address is typed at the beginning of a letter (especially if a continuation sheet is required).

Letters from Government Departments

The Civil Service lays down specific rules for the display of all typewritten matter in its official typing manual. It stresses simplification to increase productivity.

Letters are fully blocked, except where printed headings indicate otherwise (as in the address panel,

P. 3 (Cont.)

Musical Director	Nando Possi
Sketches produced by	Max Watkins
Dances arranged by	Peter Vaughan
Wardrobe Mistress	Maureen Howard
PRODUCTION BY	ERIC STRINGER
(margin straight R.H.)	(margin straight L.H)

Page 6 – Divide into six advertisement spaces & insert the following names: (top) Fredericks Furs, The Lawns Hotel; (centre) Café Continental; (bottom) Simpson's Fruiterers, Wadsons Stores (Gregsons stationers)

Page 7

at top - leave a space 2" x 2" fr. L.H. margin for photo, & on R.H. side (type) —

MARY MAUGHAN from the Emerald Isles has won the hearts of many, both on the stage & on radio. She

n/ has recently returned from the United States where she has delighted audiences from New York to Mexico, touring with the famous Pinehurst Concert Party.

In the remaining section, draw two rectangles 2" x 4" wide, & centre, under the top one: Percy Pullen & his Ensemble, & under the lower one: Doreen & her Dancers. Photos will be added later.

Pages 4 & 5 The Programme will be the 2 centre pages.

(continued)

between 1 in. parallel lines, with references and the date on the right), and open punctuation is used throughout.

The letter heading (*See* page 60 as an example) is designed so that the inside address is correctly placed to match the aperture in the standard window envelope which has been introduced for general use. In order to allow the typist to work to a single tabulation stop, the telephone extension, which is always part of the printed heading, the two references and the date, which are all in the same area as the inside address, are printed in line with each other on the right-hand side. Where appropriate the same tabular stop will serve for the beginning point of the complimentary close and designation.

Letters are typed on A4 and A5 paper, and the following general points should be noted:

a **Inside address**
- i Blocked, at the top of the letter, in the position indicated against the left-hand margin, for use with a window envelope.
- ii Full stops and commas are omitted completely.
- iii Postcodes are typed as the final line.
- iv Officially recognized abbreviations for departmental and establishment titles should normally be used in addresses instead of the full names, eg DHSS (Department of Health and Social Security), MAFF (Ministry of Agriculture, Fisheries and Food), and DE (Department of Employment).

b **References** As indicated, on the right-hand side, in the area of the inside address.

c **Date** Typed as indicated in the area of the address panel – simplified, eg 25 August 19--.

d **Margins** Usually ¾ in. on the left-hand side, one space to the right of the horizontal lines indicating the address area and ½ in. on the right-hand side.

e **Salutation** Where possible, the name is given, eg Dear Mr Brown.

f **Subject headings** To start at the left-hand margin, in full capitals, with *no* underscore, and no final full stop.

g **Text of letter**
- i Blocked style.
- ii Sub- and sub-sub-paragraphs are indented five spaces, but are always blocked, including the letters a. b. etc.
- iii Numbered paragraphs (unless specifically told to the contrary) should begin at the left-hand margin, followed by a full stop and three spaces. Sub-paragraphs to be lettered followed by a full stop and three spaces. (*Note*: Brackets are not to be used.)
- iv Punctuation – one space after a comma, two spaces after a semi-colon and colon, full stop, question and exclamation mark.
- v Figures – all numerals over ONE are typed as figures, except where a numeral is the first word of a paragraph, whether numbered or not, when it is written out in words.
- vi Recognized abbreviations are typed using open punctuation eg, ie, para, sgd, BA, NATO etc.

h **Subscription** Usually 'Yours faithfully' or 'Yours sincerely', typed either up to the left-hand margin, or at the same right-hand tabular stop as the date, etc, according to departmental preferences.

i **Name of writer** Always typed to begin at the same point as the subscription. When it is a woman, the style of address used by her should be included, without brackets.

j **Designation** Title or branch/division etc, of writer, if required, to begin immediately under and at the same point as the typed name of the writer.

k **Continuation sheet** The reverse side of the paper is used, but when more than one sheet is required, the addressee's name, reference number and date may be typed across the page from the left-hand margin (2 spaces between each group). Catchwords must not be used. Page numbers are centred at the bottom.

l **Enclosures** To be indicated by typing ENC, or ENCS followed by a figure denoting the number, at the bottom left-hand side of the letter.

m **Security classifications** To be typed in full capitals (not underscored) at the centre of the top and bottom of each page.

n **Ampersand** To be used in the names of firms and in such branch titles as O & M.

'Official letters' are now rarely used, and applicants for Civil Service posts are not expected to know how to set them out.

Foreign correspondence

Where letters in a foreign language have to be typed frequently, it is advisable to have keys fitted with accents. These are known as *'Dead keys'*, as they do not move the carriage when struck. Thus, the accent should be struck first, followed by the letter over which the accent is to appear.

Page 2

(Biographical detail on Harry Jacobs on left & leave space of 3" X 2" wide on right for photo - reverse for Glyn Williams in lower half.)

CONSERVATOIRES

HARRY JACOBS

Harry is a Devonian born & bred. He started his professional life at the age of ten when he was given the opportunity of playing Oliver Twist in a touring company. He felt drawn to the stage, studied at the Guildhall School of Music, London, & in Conservatoires in Switzerland & America.

tro/ He has played on stages in America, Austria, Africa, Australia & Germany, & has appeared many times on T.V.

caps Glyn Williams

Glyn comes from Wales. Her lovely voice, sparkling eyes & trim figure soon assured her a prominent

on/ position of the stage, both in this country & abroad. She has played in pantomime in "Jack & the Beanstalk" & in "Cinderella", has starred in and/ many summer shows in this country, as well as appearing on T.V.

Page 3

GEORGE HARRIS & NINA STRUDWICK

present

FUN

MUSIC

AND

SPECTACLE

IN

FOLIES OF THE WEST

starring:

HARRY JACOBS

GLYN WILLIAMS

MARY MAUGHAN

with

DOREEN'S DANCERS and PERCY PULLENS ENSEMBLE

(continued)

Special 'slugs' are also available to slip on to type bars, but in this case the back spacer has to be used, and therefore the general speed of typing is slower.

If accents are not provided, they should be added afterwards, preferably with a thin black ball-point pen, which approximates to the colour of the ribbon. French typewriters, however, have keys with letters and accents combined (*see* page 8).

Envelopes

As has already been mentioned (page 11) the two most popular sizes of envelope to fit the A4 and A5 paper are the C6 and the DL. Certain other envelopes are obtainable, and providing they come within the minimum and maximum sizes laid down by the Post Office Preferred Range, they may continue to be used. These sizes are: minimum 90 mm x 140 mm ($3\frac{1}{2}''$ x $5\frac{1}{2}''$); maximum – 120 mm x 235 mm ($4\frac{3}{4}''$ x $9\frac{1}{4}''$).

Window envelopes are those which have a cut-out address panel covered with a transparent material. When window envelopes are used, letters or bill heads indicate the position of the inside address, and the paper has to be folded in such a way that the inside address will show through the transparent 'window'.

When typing envelopes the following points should be noted:

1. The first line should begin just below the middle of the envelope to avoid obliteration by the Post Office franking machine, and at a point so that the completed address will look centred.

2. Whether single spacing is used depends on the size of the envelope and on individual choice. If single is not used, double spacing may be used for four or five lines, and treble spacing for three lines (although with the use of postcodes this will seldom be possible).

3. Addresses can be indented or blocked, according to choice and the size and shape of the envelope. With blocked or semi-blocked styles of letters, envelope addresses are blocked, and open punctuation is used (if it has been used in the inside address in the letter).

4. '*For the attention of . . .*', '*Confidential*', '*Private*', '*Urgent*', etc should be typed two spaces above the first line of the address, in capitals or lower case and underscored, either at the same point as the first line, or to the left of it. '*By Hand*' is typed in the top right-hand corner, in place of the stamp, so that it will not be stamped in error, or to allow the instruction to be covered by the stamp should it be found necessary to send the letter by post.

5. Each line (unless open punctuation is used) should end with a comma except the one containing the county, which will be followed by a full stop. No punctuation is used in the typing of the postcode (*See* 9 below).

6. The postal town should be in capitals.

7. The county should always be given (except as in 9 below) unless it is the same town as that of the sender. In London, the postal district or postcode should always be included.

8. When sending abroad, the country should be typed in capitals, in English terminology.

9. The characters of a postcode should never be joined, one space being left between the two groups of characters. These two groups, for sorting purposes, represent, firstly, the outward part – the town to which the letter has to be sent; secondly, the inward part – the particular area within that town to which the letter is to be delivered.

The postcode should always be the last item in an address, typed in capitals, without underlining or any punctuation whatsoever, even at the end.

Whenever possible the postcode should be on a line by itself. Where the address is long, then the county may be written on the same line as the town to allow the postcode to stand alone. Should it not be possible to occupy a line by itself, at least two spaces, but preferably six, should be left between the name of the county (or town) and the postcode.

In cities and large towns, where the postcode is applicable to, and represents that town, the county need not be included, eg DERBY, DE1 8ZL *but* HOVE, SUSSEX, BN3 8UA (in Brighton postcode area).

When sending to this country from abroad, the postcode should follow the word ENGLAND. No instructions or writing of any kind should appear below the postcode.

Large firms can apply for their own postcodes for speedier delivery.

Typists should keep up to date with the ever changing needs of Post Office mechanization. This will obviate delays in the receipt of correspondence.

10. Methods of addressing people in all walks of life are given on pages 41–2.

Chain feeding envelopes to speed the operation

Envelopes should be stacked at the left of the typewriter, inserted with the left hand and when typed removed with the right hand for stacking on the right-hand side. Block style address with single-line spacing saves time.

Task 81

Typist Will you please prepare me an 8-page programme – not the stupendous task it sounds! First, take two sheets of A4, fold in half & put one inside the other. You have 8 pages. Number consecutively in pencil. Please keep to displays suggested – but use each page to advantage.

Note: all requests for a 'space' to be replaced by a ruled box to indicate the position of a photo to be added later.

Front page (P.1)

THE CONQUEST THEATRE
TORQUAY

FOLIES

OF THE

WEST

NOTE FOLLIES

Programme 50p

Back page (P.8)

Divide into three, horizontally & centre the following names – all adverts

Trowbridge Hotel
Keat's Cavern
Watcombe Fashions

(continued)

Front feeding

1. Fix the guide for the left-hand edge of envelope and set margin stop for the average address.

2. Place envelope against paper table and twirl sharply into position for typing first line of address.

3. Type the name and address.

4. With reverse twirl, turn envelope back until the top half inch of envelope is visible. The second envelope is fed in from the front of the carriage so that the bottom edge of the second envelope is behind the top edge of the first envelope – between platen and envelope. The right hand knob is twirled with a reverse motion to bring the second envelope into the writing position. When addressed, reverse twirl to bring top edge of envelope so that the top half inch is visible, then place the next envelope in position and continue as before.

Back feeding

Insert the first envelope and bring into position for typing first line of name and address. Place the next envelope behind the inserted one. Address the first envelope, as it is rolled out roll the next one into position, then place another behind it.

Forms of address

Use of Messrs

The courtesy title of *Messrs.* should be used when addressing a partnership, except when the name of the firm is preceded by the word *The* or a title is included. Examples: *Messrs. Avis & Stokes, Messrs. Jackson & Company, The Larkswood Printing Co, Sir Henry Robinson & Co.*

A limited company is an incorporated body – a legal person, distinct from any of its members – *Messrs* should not be used before the name of a limited company. Communications should be addressed to *The Secretary*, or other official of the company, for example

The Secretary,
Larkshall Printing Works plc,
416 *Chelmsford Road,*
Brentwood, Essex,
TW5 3BL

The General Manager
Morgan & Charlton Limited
346 *Holdenhurst Road*
Southampton SO5 9QR

Mr. and Esq.

Use one *or* the other when addressing a man, never both, eg *Mr R Smith* or *R Smith, Esq.*

Initials

Typed either as *Mr. J.L. Brown* or *Mr. J. L. Brown* or *Mr J L Brown*. Letters after the name have no space between them (*See* p. 13 under 'full stop').

Decorations and Honours

Decorations or honours are arranged after the name in the following order:

*a** Those conferred by the Crown (Military, Civil decorations), eg MC, MBE
b† University degrees, eg BSc
c‡ Professional, eg FRIBA
d MP
e JP
eg *C. Hubbard, Esq., V.C., O.B.E., F.C.S., J.P.*

Sen. or Jun.

Used to distinguish between father and son. The abbreviation always follows immediately after the name, eg *A. S. Snow, Sen., Esq.* and *J. A. Snow, Jun., Esq.* (*Note* the punctuation.)

A schoolboy is addressed by his Christian and surname, eg *Donald Snow* (or preceded by 'Master').

Women

a A married woman takes her husband's Christian name, eg *Mrs John Dew.*
b A widow may still retain her late husband's initials.
c A divorcee uses her own Christian name.
d The eldest unmarried daughter of the head of the family uses the title Miss, eg *Miss M. Shaw.*
e Other unmarried daughters include their Christian names, eg *Miss Joyce Shaw.*
f A mother and unmarried daughter of the same name are addressed *Mrs F. and Miss C. Shaw.*
g A mother and unmarried daughter, where the names are different are addressed as: *Mrs A. Turner and Miss B. Bell.*
h Two unmarried daughters are addressed as: *The Misses Shaw* or *The Misses J. and M. Shaw.*

Doctors

Doctors of medicine are referred to as *Dr. Thorpe*, and envelopes are addressed *J Thorpe Esq., MD* (or *Dr J Thorpe*). If knighted, *Sir John Thorpe, MD.*

Surgeons are referred to as Mr, and addressed as *F Cory, Esq., FRCS.*

---

*(See page 32 for complete list in order of priority.)
†Except for Doctorates, degrees are usually omitted.
‡Usually omitted in private correspondence.

Task 80

Typist

Would you please ~~prepare~~ type the following programme - it will of course be stencilled later.

NEWTOWN YOUTH CLUB
Present
A CHARITY CONCERT
to be held at
The Hayward Hall, Chelmsford Rd. Canterbury
on Saturday ⸰ [Last Sat. of next month] ⸰ . 19.. at 8pm

PROGRAMME

1. Overture	Carmen	Youth Orchestra
2. Solo		Rosemarie Tipp
3. Acrobatics		Athletics Group
4. Sketch	"The Barbecue"	The Drama Group
5. Guitar Solo	Selection	Peter Jones
6. Community Songs	Selection	led by Ted Brown

(Transpose 2 and 3; Justify margin)

INTERVAL

7. Conjuring		Ben Fisher, Bob Lowe
8. Duet	"The Travellers"	Jeanne Wood, Paul Kent
9. Monologue	"The Doctor's Nightmare"	Basil Keene
10. Scottish Dancing	Selection	The Scottish Dancers
11. Music for all	Pot Pourri	Youth Orchestra
12. Puppets	"The Curtain Falls"	'The Puppeteers'

(Transpose 9 and 10)

Conductor Ted Brown
Producer John Mackinlay

Caps./ Justify/ [Instant Raffle / Sales Table] Programme 50p [Refreshments / Sweets & choc's] caps/

Title	*Address*	*Salutation*	*Complimentary Close*
Duke	His Grace the Duke of	My Lord Duke,	I remain, Your Grace's most obedient servant,
Duchess	Her Grace the Duchess of	Madam,	I remain, Your Grace's most obedient servant,
Marquess	The Most Honourable the Marquess of	My Lord Marquess,	I have the honour to be, Your obedient servant,
Marchioness	The Most Honourable the Marchioness of	Madam,	I have the honour to be, Your Ladyship's obedient servant,
Earl	The Right Honourable the Earl of	My Lord,	I have the honour to remain, your Lordship's obedient servant,
Countess	The Right Honourable the Countess of	Madam,	I have the honour to remain, your Ladyship's obedient servant,
Viscount or Baron	The Right Honourable The Viscount (The Lord)	My Lord,	I have the honour to remain, your Lordship's obedient servant,
Baronet or Knight	Sir John –, Bt (or Kt)	Sir,	I have the honour to remain, Your obedient servant,
Wife of Baronet or Knight	Lady	Madam,	I have the honour to remain, Your obedient servant,
Lord Chancellor	The Right Honourable the Lord Chancellor	My Lord,	I have the honour to remain, Your Lordship's obedient servant,
Bishop	The Right Reverend the Lord Bishop of	My Lord,	I have the honour to remain, Your Lordship's obedient servant,

Note

a I remain, We are, etc, as part of the formal complimentary close is typed one line above it and three spaces to the left.

b With kind regards, etc, is the beginning of the last paragraph and is followed by a comma.

Clergy

Clergymen are referred to as the *Vicar* (or *Rector*), or *Mr. Allen* and addressed as *The Reverend R. B. Allen* (*The Revd. R. B. Allen*) or if a Doctor of Divinity, *The Reverend R B Allen, DD* or *The Revd Dr R B Allen*. If titled, *The Rev. The Hon Richard Allen*.

An envelope addressed to a clergyman and his wife would appear: *The Revd R B and Mrs Allen.*

Note: The abbreviation 'Rev.' is frequently used.

Titled people

The correct method of addressing men and women with titles is given in brief above. A more extensive list will be found in *Titles and Forms of Address* published by A & C Black.

In these days, however, few titled people would object to simpler forms for informal purposes, eg *Dear Madam, Madam, Dear Lady Montague, Sir, Dear Lord Arundel*, etc. The complimentary close might well be: *I am, Madam, Yours faithfully/sincerely* or *I am, Sir, Yours faithfully/sincerely*, or simply, *Yours faithfully/sincerely*.

32. INT. HALL EVENING

JONATHAN is waiting impatiently for his wife. The stairs creak, he looks up & stands entranced at the elegant & unexpectedly beautiful WOMAN descending upon him.

spellbound

lc/

MELINDA

(Casually)

I hope I haven't kept you waiting long, Jonathan my dear.

(recovering his equilibrium)

JONATHAN

Darling! Is it really you? Your hair! Your dress! But - you weren't a blonde when I last saw you!

MELINDA

(maliciously)

teasingly

Wasn't I? Well, this is a day of surprises, isn't it! When we're having cocktails at the hotel I, too, will explain.

front

MELINDA walks slowly to the front door which is opened for her by her HUSBAND.

33. EXT. STREET EVENING

A CHAUFFEUR opens the ~~door of the car~~ car door as JONATHAN and MELINDA appear. Jonathan locks the door of their house, then joins his WIFE in the car.

l/c/

JONATHAN

(with a sly wink)

All set, James, for the Rendez-vous.

The car starts up, gathers speed & disappears out of sight.

NOTE: Only names are in caps - 'husband' & 'wife' should be in lc.

Postcards

a *Size*: 90 mm x 140 mm ($3\frac{1}{2}''$ x $5\frac{1}{2}''$).
b No salutation or subscription.
c No inside address (this is on the reverse side).
d Margins: About 20–25 mm ($\frac{3}{4}''$ to $1''$), depending on content.
e Reference and date are generally on the same line at the top, under the address.
f If there is no reference the date can be typed at the bottom left-hand side.

Postcards are used for personal and business correspondence when the message is short and not of a private nature.

Firms usually have their address printed at the top, but if this is to be typed, the neatest, most economical style is to centre it at the top, on one line, or two at the most, with a line ruled one space down, right across the card.

Memorandum forms

The memorandum (or memo) is used for internal communications or for sending messages to representatives or agents of the firm.

a Paper – any size can be used, according to the length of the message, but A5 (landscape) is that most used.
b Heading – Memorandum.
c In the upper section, often above a line ruled across: To From Date Ref (if required).
d Lower section, below the line, contains the message and signature, and designation if required.
e There is no salutation or subscription.

```
MEMORANDUM

To    All members of the Staff          Date   9 March 19--

From  Mr B A Brown, Supervisor          Ref    BAB/PS/FA/7

_____________________________________________________________

REST ROOM

It may not be generally known that there is a comfortably furnished room
with a bed and easy chairs which may be used by any member of staff who
is feeling ill. The key is kept by the Librarian and may be obtained at
anytime.

If a member of staff does feel unwell, however, he/she should notify me
or my deputy so that we are aware of the situation.
```

```
MEMORANDUM
Mr S Fiddler
Communications Manager

1 July 19--

NEW STYLE STATIONERY


Your comments regarding the proposed new design of our stationery have
been noted. As soon as the alterations have been made I will send you
a proof copy for your further inspection and approval.

With regard to the publicity leaflet to be sent to America, this should
be ready in a day or two.




A B Scott
Manager
Design Department

ref ABS/CD 324/C
```

Miss Smith.
Please continue this film script begun yesterday.

16.

30. EXT. GARDEN LATE AFTERNOON

MELINDA is sitting and enjoying the peace and beauty of her trim little garden, when the sudden appearance of her HUSBAND rouses her from her reveries. lc/

MELINDA
Darling! What is the matter? Aren't you well?

JONATHAN
Well? Well? - Well off, my little Lindy.

MELINDA
(Taken aback)
You haven't called me that for years!

JONATHAN
(Ignoring the remark)
We're going out to have a fabulous evening. Come on; no questions. The car's ordered - the table's booked - and we've got to get changed.

Speechless, MELINDA follows her HUSBAND into the house.

31. INT. BEDROOM LATE AFTERNOON

MELINDA sits on the bed and looks at her HUSBAND defiantly.

MELINDA
Jonathan, I won't move until you tell me what you're up to. You've a wicked twinkle in your eyes!

JONATHAN
When we're having cocktails at the hotel I will explain. The car is ordered for 6.30 - so get weaving!

(continued)

Many firms now use a blocked style of memorandum form, omitting the headings *To From* and *Subject*.

The name of the addressee appears at the top, with the designation following the signature at the bottom. The reference will also appear at the foot of the page.

The two methods of display are given. If more than the name is to be typed (eg department, or address in the case of representatives) the second display would be preferable.

Compliments slip

This is a communication sent with leaflets, etc, when no message is required.

It is usually printed on A6 (half A5) paper, used either way round and contains the words '*With the Compliments of*' followed by the name of the firm or association. If '*With the Compliments of the Secretary*' is used, then the name and address of the Association will generally be given.

Telephone messages

As it is imperative that telephone messages are passed on accurately and speedily, message pads are usually kept beside the telephone. The layout can be in any style, providing the following information is included:

a Name of person for whom the call is intended.
b Name of caller.
c Telephone number of caller.
d Message.
e Time and date of call.
f Signature of person taking the call.

When giving the message, it is clearer if broken up, each point being given a new paragraph.

Sometimes the pad is used only for quick notes at the time of the call, and the message is typed to await the executive on his return. It is recommended that A5 or A6 paper be used, and a suggested display is given on page 45. This form can also be used for personal callers. (*See* page 45 for an example of a typed message.) To ensure that telephone messages receive priority treatment they can be typed on coloured paper, and should be placed either in a distinctive folder, or clipped to a coloured board – in each case marked 'Telephone Messages'.

Special care should be taken that dates, times, and names are accurate and should be repeated for the caller to check. Should any letter or letters be indistinct, the Post Office Telephone Alphabet should be used.

Telephone alphabet

A	for	Andrew	N	for	Nellie
B	"	Benjamin	O	"	Oliver
C	"	Charlie	P	"	Peter
D	"	David	Q	"	Queenie
E	"	Edward	R	"	Robert
F	"	Frederick	S	"	Samuel
G	"	George	T	"	Tommy
H	"	Harry	U	"	Uncle
I	"	Isaac	V	"	Victor
J	"	Jack	W	"	William
K	"	King	X	"	X-ray
L	"	Lucy	Y	"	Yellow
M	"	Mary	Z	"	Zebra

Telemessages – inland and international

Telemessage is an electronic mail service. Any message phoned in by 10 pm (7 pm on Sundays) is delivered by post the next working day (including Saturdays) – typed on an A4 sheet and enclosed in a large distinctive yellow and blue envelope.

The Telemessage Service is obtained via the telephone operator or through telex. The price is based on the number of words in the message (in groupings of 50 words), the addressee's name and address and punctuation being free of charge.

Telemessage offers other facilities, eg Multiple Messages, Direct Response, Sender's Copy and Special Occasion Cards (with a variety of illustrations).

A file copy of the full text should be kept, with a note of the date and time sent. If a complete letter is to be dictated, the copy should be typed in the usual way, with paragraphs and punctuation (as little as possible) for easy dictation.

International telegrams

International telegrams may be sent to most countries, via the operator or through telex. There is a standing charge, and then each word is charged for individually, including names and addresses, but punctuation is free.

```
Telegram despatched: 12.6.--
                     1405 hrs

Robinson
75 Burgerstrasse
ZURICH
Switzerland

Arriving Tuesday 1640 hrs Meet
at airport

                          Turner
```

ACT ONE Scene One

The drawing-room of the Manners' Home. WENDY CRABBE /l.c and PENNY MANNERS are looking through a large picture window on to the garden.

ℓ. WENDY Penny! – I don't know how you + Benders ever managed it; it's the loveliest garden I know of. How did you do it?

l.c./ PENNY Work, dear. (W. What, dear? P. Work)

WENDY oh!

PENNY And quite a lot of it, too.

W. You've got a second pigeon now I see.

P. Yes, though strictly speaking we didn't get her, I mean. Perky got her for himself a couple of days ago. She's French, or so Tiddly Tite says.

W. How does he know whether a bird is French or not?

P. (moving over towards an easy chair) I don't know, but he says he's kept birds all his life.

W. (sitting on a chair by the window) That I can well believe!

P. Pigeons, dear, not the other kind!

W. How do you know?

P. Ben told me, (because when Perky moved in on us + wouldn't go away, Ben) went over to Tiddly's bar + asked his advice.

W. Any excuse!

P. Well, you know what men are when they get together over a drink.

W. Don't I just!

P. Anyway, that's what Ben came home with; that, + some food for them.

W. Talking of food, just look at those two pigeons ~~eating~~ gobbling up their dinner, you'd think they were starving.

P. Tiddly says they are homing birds, resting up before completing their journey home.

W. Tiddly says! The only thing I trust about that sailorman is his nickname Tiddly – it suits him.

P. Yes, doesn't it, but it doesn't mean what you think it means.

l.c./ W. I might have known that! I've always thought 'Tiddly' meant having had too much to drink.

v.c./ P. So it does, Wendy, but not in the navy. Apparently, when you call a sailor 'tiddly' it means the same as 'dandy', very/ someone who is particular about his appearance.

W. Well, that's true enough, he is.

P. Oh, good, the kettle is boiling. (She goes out to make tea.)

Mr. Franklin

The Area Manager telephoned to say that he would be visiting this district next week and would like to speak to you on an important matter regarding the new sales drive.

Would you please phone him during the afternoon as he would like to know which day would be most convenient to you. His number is:

01-432 0324

B Smith

1515 hrs.

12 July 19--

Example of a telephone message typed on A6 paper.

MESSAGE SHEET

Telephone/Personal Visit

Time received: ________ Date: __________

Message for: ______________________

Caller's name: ______________________

Address: ______________________

____

____

Tel. No: ______________________

Message: ______________________

____

____

____

____

____

____

(Signed) ______________________

Typing the correspondence

In the typing of the correspondence that follows, it is hoped that students will treat it realistically by taking the usual carbon copies for filing purposes and when possible typing envelopes.

The general display suggested should be followed, instructions must be carried out, and consistency should be maintained, but it is up to the student to choose the size of paper, the width of margins, and general positioning on the paper according to the length of the letter. Where correspondence consists of several pages it is important to read the whole document and relevant notes before starting to type.

All correspondence should be dated, and when, within the correspondence, a reference only is made to a date, the date should be given to correspond with that on which the particular letter etc, is actually typed.

References should be included where given, and in addition the initials of the employer (the member of staff concerned) and the typist.

If required any of the following traditional style letters may be typed as blocked or semi-blocked for extra practice in these styles.

Memorandums should be typed as appropriate, or according to the 'Rules of the House'.

In the typing of postcards, if these are not available A6 paper may be used.

All spelling and other obvious errors should be corrected and the correspondence presented ready for signature.

Task 78

Typist This new Comedy in 3 acts by A. Gausden is to be sent to a producer in Sussex as soon as possible. Please make a start on the Title Page, etc.

BIRDS OF A FEATHER

Characters

③ WENDY CRABBE ~~friend of~~ her friend
② PENNY MANNERS ~~wife of~~ his wife
① BENTLEY 'BENDERS' MANNERS Ben to his wife
Chou-Chou a bird-fancying cat
caps Perky } both pigeons the bird fancied
& Co. Perky's friend
TIDDLY TITE a former sailor & now landlord of 'The Jolly Tar Inn'
JACK KIPPER R.N. a sailor in the Queen's Navee
ADMIRAL IRONBITER another sailor in the Queen's Service
CAPTAIN BROADSIDE ship's parrot
'YOU KNOW WHO' a lady of principle

SYNOPSIS OF ^ACTS AND^ SCENES

The action of the play takes place in the drawing-room of the Manners's home

Time: the present

ACT ONE

scene One An afternoon in summer
scene Two Evening, the same day

ACT TWO

scene One Noon the following day
" Two The same night

ACT THREE

scene One Early evening a week later
Two A few hours later.

(continued)

Task 16

Typist a) Letter to Mr. Brooks (add Ref. AC/C/176)
b) Similar letter to Mr. F.M. Gee, 68 Goodwin Rd. Manchester, M30 8QR, re Mr. R. Sawyer of 31 Westhill Rd. Solihull, West Midlands. (Block + open punctuation)

Tomorrow's date please

Confidential

R. Brooks, Esq.,
5 Smithy Street,
Ashby-De-La-Zouche,
Leics. LE6 5ZA

Dear Mr. Brooks,

Mr. John Gibson

Mr. John Gibson of 27 Heatherston Road, Birmingham, has applied for credit with our firm and has given your name as a reference.

I should be grateful if you would answer the following questions about the applicant -

1. How long have you known Mr. Gibson, and is he still a customer of yours?

2. ~~Having~~ With regard to his payments -

   (i) Does he always pay his bills promptly?

   (ii) Does a reminder have to be sent?

   ~~(ii)~~ (iii) Has he ever asked for an extension of the period of payment, and if so, how many times?

3. ~~Do~~ Would you consider him a good, fair, or poor risk, if we were to grant him credit?

If you have any other information about Mr. Gibson's credit standing we shall, of course, be glad to have it. I enclose a s.a.e. (in full) for your reply.

Anything you tell us will be kept strictly confidential, and, if at any time we can help you in a similar manner, we will gladly do so.

Yours ~~faithfully~~ sincerely,
HEPWORTH & MAY PLC (caps)

Manager

(3)

CAMS: 3C, 1C

(3 spaces) 4" (2)

FADE IN — 3. INT. (3) SITTING ROOM OF REDMAYES — /BOOM A 1/

60. 3 C

M2-s HILLARY/IVY

(4)

(WE OPEN ON HILLARY AND IVY GAZING OUT OF THE OPEN WINDOW ON TO A GARDEN ABLAZE WITH COLOUR) ←1"→

(4)

IVY: I wonder whether they really will leave Redmayes. Jack loves it here.

(2)

HILLARY: But Amelia is strongly in favour of buying Cedar Hall ---/

61. 1 C

M2-s AMELIA/JACK

(THE DOOR OPENS. JACK AND A JUBILANT AMELIA COME IN)

AMELIA: There - we've done it!

62. 3 C — JACK: Yes, we really have./

M2-s HILLARY/IVY

HILLARY: You mean you've decided to buy Cedar Hall?

Pull back to M4-s JACK/AMELIA/IVY/HILLARY

(AMELIA NODS)

I'm so glad for you, as I know you'd set your heart on it.

IVY: Yes, I'm delighted, and I'm sure, Jack, that you will love it. It really is a most beautiful house, and the garden is fantastic!

(JACK COMES OVER TO AMELIA)

When do you expect to go in?

JACK: If it's ready, by the end of October.

IVY: Is there much to be done to get it as you want it?

JACK: Oh, a tremendous amount - but then, there usually is when you move

63. 1 C — to a new house./

M2-s JACK/AMELIA

AMELIA: Especially to the decorations - that's my province, and I'm so looking forward to it.

Pan AMELIA down

(3 NEXT)

Typist: Please type for a Miss Richards who wants to see how a script for TV is displayed.

Task 17

Typist This letter to go to Mr T. Murray, Man. Dir. of Excelsior Secretarial Services Bureau Ltd: George St London W1H 5PN 1+2 (1 for Mrs Bryant of information)

Dear Mr Murray,

Having spent 4 days at yr Sec. Ser. Bureau in Bromley I have pleasure in sending you my report.

In view of the fact that the Bureau has bn in op. for such a short time you have every reason to be optimistic about the future.

Staff [I shd like to pay tribute to yr Supervisor, Mrs Quickenden, who has all the qualities for a person who holds such a position, & she is undoubtedly dedicated to her role of making a success of her department

only/ It is essential to have ~~first-class~~ staff. fr the point of view of operational skills & also their personality

trs/ & approach to the public. Those you have already appear in every way suitable & I detect an excellent rapport with

NP Mrs Q. [If there is to be further expansion, however, I wd suggest that more than one op. of the word processor is necy, & other staff might need to be taken on as a result of my comments on equipment.

considerable I believe there is potential in the area for legal work, with several young solicitors starting up on their own & unable to afford the necy staff & expensive equipment. For this you would need to appoint an experienced legal sec. who could take full responsibility for that side of the work. She would need a W.P. for her own use & should be expected to deal direct with the solicitors or their representatives in complete confidentiality.

Equipment I would suggest the purchase of a further W.P. (for the legal section) + another electronic typewriter. Your reprographic section with photocopier & offset litho is well equipped & you shd be able to deal with any request & execute the work efficiently.

(continued)

1. VOICE: Poor devils!

2. SUSAN: (*with concern*) But the men were not on the boats were they?

3. VOICE: (*talking to himself*) Two life boats have got away — but I haven't seen the third again. I wonder - - -

4. 2nd VOICE: What the so-&-so's going on over there? As if there's not enough trouble already.

5. SUSAN (anxiously looking round) Oh, Phil, where are you?

6. POLICEMAN (sternly) Make way there. Keep this entrance free — we've more casualties than we can cope with.

(THE SOUND OF VOICES CEASES & THERE IS SUDDEN SILENCE.)

You, Miss, come & give a hand, there's someone needs assistance, & we can't spare anyone from the ambulance at the moment, it's down by the water's edge. Yes, just down here.

(A muffled scream is heard)

(Calling & pushing her way through the crowd) Phil! Phil!

7. SUSAN Phil! Oh, no! It can't be true!

Typist Correct wrong spacing after characters on previous page.

There is, however, one major omission – you have no audio machines. These would bring you into direct contact with firms whose executives dictate ~~their work~~ on to cassettes. You wd have a ready market, especially when their staff are away unexpectedly.
correspondence & reports.

Clientele

Whilst I wd advocate good publicity, it is by recommendation that you will attract a wide clientele.

The following are the type of people for whom you wd expect to cater.

(6) 1. Individuals who call fr time to time – mainly fr photocopying.
(5) 2. Societies, where the sec is unable to carry out all the necy typ. & dup. – in connection with meetings & the organisation of conferences & dinners.
nc/
(2) 3. Businesses where there are problems (either with) holidays & illness depleting their staff.
(3) 4. Offices where staffing has bn reduced, & the services of the Bureau might be used on a permanent basis.
(4) 5. Young solicitors starting up on their own or with another young partner.
(8) 6. Writers of every kind, including script writers fr TV & Radio
(7) 7. Lecturers for Colleges, & Professional Speakers.
(1) 8. Businesses wh the production of booklets etc ~~are~~ is frequent.

I have, of course, discussed these points with Mrs Q. who is fully aware of the needs / & the great potential of the Bureau. /of,

T/

If I can be of any futher assistance please do not hesitate to contact me.

Yours sincerely

John M. Taylor
Consultant

note: Please put in the order of the encircled numbers.

Task 76

Typist. Here is the next part of the new radio play "The Wrecks" by E. Rich.

- 9 -

1. SUSAN: (Calling through the storm) Coooeee ... Phil are you there? Oh, I thought I'd lost you.

2. PHIL: I was trying to get a better look at the wreck.

3. SUSAN: (Very excited) Oh, Phil, what a storm! I've never really been in an 'Incident' before. Look! There's another life-boat coming round the point.

4. POLICEMAN: (In a commanding voice) Stand clear please - the ambulance is on its way.

5. SUSAN: Did he say 'Ambulance'? Oh, Phil! How marvellous! I've never seen one in action. Is it true there are two wrecks?

6. PHIL: (Trying to sound calm) Now calm yourself down, Susan, or you'll be needing the ambulance.

(THE SOUND OF THE AMBULANCE GROWS NEARER)

7. SUSAN: (Almost shouting in her exuberance) Oh, this is the most exciting day I've ever had. I've never seen such crowds.

8. VOICE: (Crossly) You wouldn't say that if you were involved, instead of being a spectator.

9. SUSAN: (In a surprised tone of voice) But of course not! I'm enjoying it now because I can look on, it's like taking part in a film. I saw one very like this a couple of weeks back. Oh, what was that awful bang? It sounded like an explosion.

10. VOICE: (As though he expected it) That's one of them gone up. I wonder how long now.

11. SUSAN: (Incredulously) One what? How long for what?

12. VOICE: (Dryly) One of the tankers. The other one won't be long now.

(A SERIES OF BANGS IS HEARD)

(continued)

Typist Please type this letter ready for signature when I come back late to-day.

Ref. NB/I/96

C. E. Williams
599 Commercial Rd
Portsmouth,
PO2 7AN

Dear Mr. Williams

Thank you very much for yr. enquiry received yesterday regarding the advisability of opening a new furniture store in Portsmouth & the possibility of our supplying you with merchandise. It is a pleasure to be able to assist you in establishing yr new furniture store.

In answer to yr question about a desirable location, I have 3 5 suggestions that may be of value to you.

5/

change the order but keep numbers

2 1. Try to obtain a position that is near or on the main business street.

3 2. If possible, locate yr store near or on a bus route.

5 3. If you plan to build yr own building, make sure the site you purchase or lease is large enough for future expansion.

4. Make sure the store has ample parking space nearby.

1. Try to locate yr. store in a relatively new suburb or section of the city that is growing in population.

Regarding the possibility of stocking our household furniture, we shall be pleased to

(continued)

Task 75

Typist – Please make a copy of the following – times have to be checked and then you can type the stencil later.

CAMERA SCRIPT

PROGRAMME NO. (1234/5678)

"THE DROP OUTS"

by

treble

MARY SHEPPEY

Producer .... William Armstrong
Director .... Charles Travers
Story Editor .... David Roberts
P.A. .... Norman Truman
F.M. .... James Body
A.F.M. .... Cyril Johns
F.A. .... Alfred Goodman

=

Designer .... Clifford Stuart
Costume Supervisor .... Sheila Mitchell
Make-up Supervisor .... Joy Towner

=

T.O.M.1 .... Robert Tripp
T.O.M.2 .... Eric Langford
Sound Supervisor .... Richard Burley
Crew .... Eight
treble Vision Mixer .... Denise Watson

2" margin

these names in caps. please

roughly 2" margin

in full

CAMERA REHEARSAL. STUDIO BD1. ~~8th~~ 10 + ~~9th~~ 11 FEB. 19--

Tuesday, 10th Feb.

1430 – 1900 Camera Rehearsal
1900 – 2000 DINNER
2000 – 2215 Camera Rehearsal

=

Wednesday, 11th Feb.

=

1000 – 1200 Camera Rehearsal
1200 – 1300 LUNCH
1300 – 1730 Camera Rehearsal
1730 – 1845 DINNER
1845 – 1915 Line-up

=

1915 – 2130 RECORD

=

2130 – 2200 RECORD – SOUND RETAKES

1½" margin

Note
Single spacing throughout, double where indicated thus =

supply you with our complete range of items. We are
k-day / sending you our latest catalogue in which you will
(wholesale) will find descriptions, illustrations & prices of every piece
& suite of furniture we manufacture. Although you
may sell Mansfield furniture at any price you wish,
our catalogue contains a suggested retail price list
that many retailers find helpful to follow.

Add "A" — As you plan to open a new business, you may not
want wish to stock all the pieces & suites we manufacture.
We therefore suggest the following items because many
retailers find them to be popular with their customers.
Descriptions of each suite or individual pieces appear
in our catalogue on the pages indicated.

Please use block style.

Living Room furniture - Pages 15-30
Item numbers: 366, 368, (399, 381), 400, 406-18

Dining Room furniture - Pages 37-52
← Item numbers: 488, 490, 494, 499, 501, 407-39

Bedroom furniture - Pages 56-68 9
← Item numbers: 451, 453, 455, 458-66

Kitchen furniture - Pages 73-8
Item numbers: 80, 82, 84-100

Misc. Items - Pages 82-9
Item numbers: 105, 108, 109, 111, 123, 136-40

Will you please fill in the enclosed credit
application form & return it to us. As soon as we
have the necessary credit information about yr. new business we shall be pleased to open an account
for you, & be ready to send you yr. first consignment.

We extend to you our very best wishes for the success
of yr new business, & if we can be of further assistance
please do not hesitate to contact us.

Yrs. sinc.

Sales Manager

(continued)

Caps   Act Two

(small) [The] Drawing-room at Hunstanton Chase after dinner. The lamps are lit. MRS. ALLONBY, MRS LADY STUTFIELD & LADY HUNSTANTON are seated on the sofa, with LADY CAROLINE ↗ PONTEFRACT in a chair beside them.

In a corner of the room behind them, MISS HESTER WORSLYE is sitting inconspicuously pretending to read a book.

MRS. ALLONBY — What a comfort it is to have got rid of the men for a little!

LADY STUTFIELD — Yes; men persecute us dreadfully, don't they?

MRS. AL. — Persecute us? I wish they did.

LADY H. — My dear!

MRS. A. — The annoying thing is that the wretches can be perfectly happy without us. That is why I think it is every woman's duty never to leave them alone for a single moment, except during this short breathing space after dinner, without which, I believe we poor women would be absolutely worn to shadows.

(small) Enter SYDNEY & other SERVANTS with coffee

LADY H. — Worn to shadows, dear?

MRS. A. — Yes, Lady Hunstanton. It is such a strain keeping men up to the mark. They are always trying t escape from us.

LADY S. — It seems to me that it is we who are always trying t escape from them. Men are so very, very heartless. They know their power & use it.

LADY CAROLINE — (takes coffee from SYDNEY) What stuff & nonsense all this about men is! The thing to do is to keep men in their proper place.

MRS. A. — But what is their proper place, Lady Caroline?

LADY C. — Looking after their wives, Mrs. A.

MRS. A. — (takes coffee from servant) Really? And if they're not married?

(Send a copy of this letter to Mr J.C. please)

P.S. As our Area Representative, Mr. John Crowther, will be in Portsmouth next week I will ask him to call on you.

A at the outset. As yr business develops, however, you might like to increase yr range of furniture.

Typist - Will you please draft me out a new "Application for Credit" form — this will, of course, have to be duplicated afterwards. The information required will be:

Name of applicant: — — — —
Address — —
Name of new business — —
Address — —
Telephone —
Type of business
Areas of other branches
Date firm first established
Bank
Names & addresses of 2 referees
Signature & position in firm

(Display attractively - but economically)

Task 74

Typist - Here is the first part of Act Two of "A Woman of No Importance" which you began last week for the local Rep. Now that the cast has been selected, will you please type the necessary pages as well, in correct style.

Title Page

A Woman ---

A Comedy
in
Four Acts
by
Oscar Wilde

SYNOPSIS OF ACTS & SCENES

Act One	The lawn in front of the terrace at Hunstanton Chase
Act Two	The drawing-room at H.C. after dinner.
Three	The Picture Gallery at H.C.
Four	The sitting-room at Mrs. Arbuthnot's house at Wrockley.

CHARACTERS & CAST

Lord Illingworth	- Dennes Pownall
Lady Hunstanton	- Katie Buckland
Sir John Pontefract	- John Fisher
Lady Caroline Pontefract	- Patricia Matlock
Lord Alfred Rufford	- Terry Clark
Lady Stutfield	- Olivia Scot
Mr. Kelvil, M.P.	- Val Woodland
The Ven. Archdeacon Daubeny, DD	- Francis Bentley
Gerald Arbuthnot	- George Duntler
Mrs. Arbuthnot	- Violet Goddard
Mrs. Allonby	- Sarah Green
Miss Hester Worslye	- Molly Grey
Farquhar, Butler	- Peter Pointer
Francis, Footman	- Robin Punter
Alice, Maid	- Norah Pritchard

(continued)

Task 19

Your Ref. RC/32/4/BA/CS
Our Ref. SED/PW/RC/3

Messrs. Brown & Peters,
Upper Charleston Road,
Manchester.
M16 7RW

Please re-type with amendments + additions - + mark for the attention of Mrs. F. Healar.

Dear Sirs,

Reconstruction of Canteen

Further to our recent discussions regarding the reconstruction of our canteen, I have studied the suggested plan which you kindly prepared for me. In the main I think it would suit our purposes very well, but there are certain ~~comments~~ points I should like to ~~make~~ comment on.

THE OFFICE. This appears a little "out of touch" with the rest of the working quarters. The adminstration of a canteen of this size entails a great deal of office work, and I feel the Supervisor's office should be in such a position that she can see not only the whole of the kitchen but also the dining room.

Add 'A' →

THE WASHING-UP SECTION. Considerably more thought is needed. I have not decided whether the semi-automatic or the fully automatic dishwasher will best suit our purpose. I should like to see both of these in action before I make ~~my~~ the final decision.

THE SERVICE COUNTER. This, of course, is the focal point in the dining room, and seems ideal. I like the idea of a hot cupboard with the sliding doors to keep the heat in, in addition to the hot-water well below.

Add 'B' →

EQUIPMENT. In addition to the large equipment I shall need a certain amount of smaller items to supplement those we already have. From your catalogue I have selected a few items I should like to purchase straight away. Would you please confirm that you have them in stock, and that these are the current prices.

No.	789	Baking sheet	50 cm x 40 cm x 2 cm	£5.10
	791	Pie dish	45 cm x 35 cm x 8 cm	£6.00
	792	Baking dish	40 cm x 30 cm x 7 cm	£6.50
	801	Plate cover	21 cm diameter x 5 cm	£1.45
	833	Service trays	32 cm x 25 cm	£2.15
	846	Wooden trays	42 cm x 32 cm	£1.10

I shall look forward to hearing from you within the course of the next few days.

Yours faithfully,
PETERSON & STRATFORD COMPANY LIMITED

S.E. Davies
General Manager

See over

(continued)

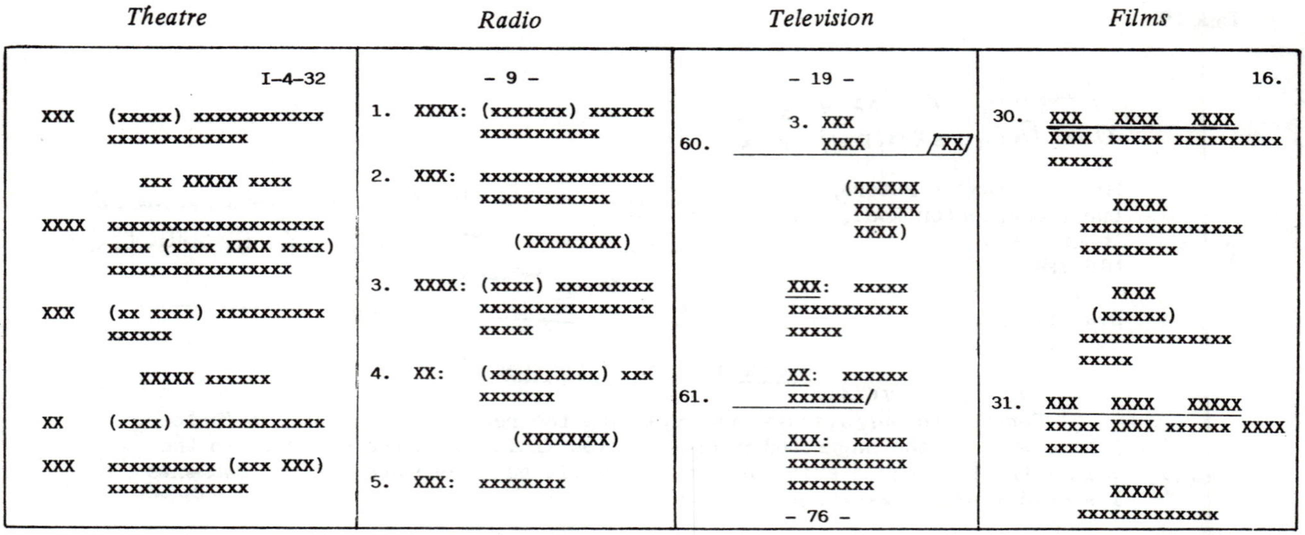

Diagrammatic chart showing the basic differences in display of the four entertainment media

Notes

Radio being an entirely aural medium, relies on sound effects to assist in producing and interpreting the visual scenes in the listener's mind, in the same way that the intonation of the voice indicates the mood and temperament of the characters.

As performances are given in front of a microphone, the layout of the script is of vital importance to assist easy reading, so professionally pica type is used, and pages are attached at the top left-hand corner. The importance of page turnover is stressed by the fact that spacing at the end of the page is secondary to completing a speech, or at least a sentence.

Television scripts comprise not only the dialogue, with its dependent directions, but also directions for sound effects and the cameras. These must be clearly shown, hence the typing in two columns. The 'shots' are numbered at 1 in., and ruled off across the page to end with an oblique stroke in line with the final words of the last speaker.

Note the pagination. Numbers are centred over the page, 1 in. from the top and bottom, but as most drama scripts are recorded out of sequence these numbers will usually differ. At the top the numbers run continuously in the final viewing order; at the bottom the numbers refer to the order in which the script is going to be recorded.

Rehearsal scripts for actors contain only the dialogue and relevant directions, but the 4 in. margin is maintained.

Film scripts have a similarity in structure to those for both television and the theatre – cameras are used as in the former and therefore 'set' directions are used, and for clarity and uniformity there are three main 'stops', as in the latter.

Programmes vary considerably in their display, depending on the event and the presentation of the items; they can be single sheets, or the more elaborate 4–, 6– or 8–page leaflet. Centred and blocked styles may be mixed, and justified left- and right-hand margins and boxes give variety to highlight names and focus attention on special parts of the programme – or merely produce an attractive display.

Typing of scripts

The following scripts and programmes should be displayed attractively, due attention being paid to any specific instructions given, or typed according to the indications given above.

Task 19 (continued)

"A" THE STAFF ROOM. There does not seem to be adequate space allocated to it to contain the necessary number of lockers - unless you suggest putting them elsewhere.

'B' WATER BOILERS. The range of these is so vast I have not yet decided which ^are^ to install. I shall be visiting several canteens within the next week & will then discuss the matter again with you.

Typist Please send a memo to Mrs. F. Walker, Canteen Superviser, suggesting she might like to accompany me when I visit the large canteen in Spears & Webbs next Wed. & send her a copy of this letter.

Task 20

This letter is to go to Mr. B. Tanner & addressed Poste Restante, Bureau de Poste, Berne, Switzerland.

Dear Mr. Tanner,

Thank you for your letter received this morning. The address you wanted is: Monsieur F. Schultz, 267 Brunnadernestrasse, Kirchenfeld, Berne. [Display address clearly]

I am ~~so~~ very/ glad your tour has been so successful & I hope that business will continue to flourish.

Everything seems to be well under control here in your absence, I am, however, enclosing a letter which I think you should see. Perhaps you will let me know what you would like me to do about it when you send the next tape.

Tape No. 2 has been received & all the letters have been duly dealt with.

With kind regards,

Yours sincerely,

Television

Scripts for television are typed in two columns, visual on the left and audio on the right. It is often required to type only the audio, but a wide left-hand margin must still be allowed for the camera instructions.

Characters' names begin at 4 in., are typed in capitals underscored, and followed by a colon.

Main margin is also at 4 in.

Dialogue begins on the same line as the name of the character, or at the margin on the next line down.

Spacing is generally single, with treble between speeches.

Directions are typed in capitals and enclosed within brackets. When referring to characters other than the one speaking, directions are inset 1 in. from the margins, in single spacing, with 4 clear spaces left before them.

Pagination. Numbers are typed 1 in. from the top *and* bottom, centred over the page (*see* page 109).

Camera instructions. Each 'shot' is numbered and ruled off, with special instructions typed above and below the line, in the left-hand margin. Visual instructions must coincide with the audio character instructions. ('Shot' numbers are at 1 in. from the edge of the paper.)

Films

Margins and stops. Set directions – $1\frac{1}{2}$ in. from the edge of the paper. General directions – $1\frac{1}{2}$ in., right-hand margin $\frac{1}{2}$ to 1 in. Dialogue (First Stop) – 3in., right-hand margin $1\frac{1}{2}$ in. Character directions (Second Stop) – 4 in. Character names – $4\frac{1}{2}$ in.

Spacing is single throughout with double between speeches and before and after general directions.

Characters' names are typed in capitals all beginning at the same point – $4\frac{1}{2}$ in.

Dialogue (First Stop) begins *immediately* under the name of the character (one space down) unless separated from it by character directions and blocked.

Set directions. Each scene is numbered, followed at $1\frac{1}{2}$ in. in capitals by:

a INT (or EXT) to indicate whether interior or exterior scene.
b Location.
c Time of day.

General directions at $1\frac{1}{2}$ in. are those which come at the beginning of scenes describing the scenes, referring to characters not at the moment speaking, giving a description of the character about to speak, and camera directions. This is all typed in single spacing, blocked in lower case with characters referred to (and often camera directions) in capitals.

Character directions. Short directions referring to a character's speech are typed between the name of the character and the speech (in single spacing), enclosed within brackets and beginning with a small letter. This position is known as the Second Stop.

Pagination. Numbers are typed at the top right-hand side.

Scenes are numbered consecutively throughout the script; a brief description (internal or external, place, time) being typed in capitals, separated by stops or three spaces, and sometimes underscored (*see* page 118).

Programmes

Theatre programmes vary according to individual preferences. It is the standard practice in printing of presenting the names of the characters in lower case, with the cast in capitals. This is usually followed in typewritten work with a justified margin.

Concert programmes

There are two recognized methods of display. The first has *three columns*. The left-hand column states the type of item (with or without a number); the second column is centred on the page, and contains the title of the item; the third column, with a straight right-hand margin, gives the name of the performer.

The second method contains *two columns*. The first gives the item, subdivided if necessary, and the second column gives the composer's name justified at the right-hand margin. In this case the artists' names usually appear at the head of the programme.

Typist — Will you please make me a draft of this circular letter as it will appear in its final form. Put my address at the top of course, and "Date as Postmark".

Dear

in full the / stet

Will you help me gather some information ~~re~~ about the (T.V.) habits of people living in your immediate vicinity? ~~neighbourhood~~

It will take a few minutes (only) of your time, but the answers you ~~will~~ give will be very important to me, as they will be used as data for a research

N.P. project I am conducting. [Please write your answers against the questions at the foot of this letter, tear the slip off & send it in the

s.a. enclosed envelope.

run on (Your co-operation will be very much appreciated.

Yours sincerely,

— — — — — — — — — — — — — — — — — —

Miss S. Garratt, 35 Branksome Ave. Poole, Dorset BH15 4DW

Television Viewing

1. Approx. how many hours a week do you & your family ~~use the~~ watch T.V.? - - - - - - - - - -
2. Which channel do you & yr. family tune in to most frequently? - - - - - - - -
3. Which programme is enjoyed most
   (i) by you - - - - - - - -
   (ii) by yr. children - - - - - - -
   (iii) by yr. husband - - - - - -

   change round

4. If you have a "pet peeve" regarding television programmes, will you explain it briefly - - -

leave more space here

(Please spread out & display attractively) (Name of Road) - - - - - -

speaking are typed at the Direction Stop (as in 4 above).
6 If short directions within brackets do not constitute a sentence, no full stop is used.

Ruling

1 Unspoken words *may* be underlined if required by individual producers.
2 Characters' names are not underlined when this is to be done by the actors to identify their own parts (see Actor's script).

First three pages

Everything should be centred on each page (after allowing for binding). These pages are not usually numbered.

1 Title Page (Title, Drama/Comedy, Number of Acts, Author).
2 Characters' names – in capitals, with any descriptions, eg 'a friend of the family' in lower case. Double-line spacing; single and blocked if the description takes more than one line. (The cast cannot be given in an *original* typing of a play, but can be included only after the parts have been allocated by the producer. *Then*, the names of characters are in lower case and the names of the cast are in capitals.)
3 Synopsis of Acts, Scenes, Scene settings and time. The style of typing the Acts and Scenes should be similar to that used throughout the play.

Note: Should the number of characters be small, the Synopsis of Acts, etc, can all be put on the same page.

Descriptions of costumes, where applicable, and detailed plan/s, etc of the stage, are usually given at the end of the typescript.

Cover

It is common practice to have a 'window' cut in the front cover, about a quarter of the way down, to allow the title of the play on the title page to be visible.

Actor's script

An actor is normally given the script of the whole play from which to work. In order to identify his own part, he usually underlines the name of the character he is to play.

Actor's part

This consists of a portion of a play given to an actor who has only a small part, ie the appropriate pages from the typescript of the complete play.

The 'Cue Script' or 'Actor's part' which introduced the characters by having leader dots and cues is currently in most places being superseded by the type which includes at least five speeches before his entrance, and the entire script, intact, until his exit. Should his entry be at the beginning of an Act, then he would also receive the scene directions as in the complete play. In a professional company the actor would receive the typescript for the entire Scene/s in which he appeared.

The cover containing this actor's part will give the name of the play, the author and the words: 'Acting part for . . .'.

Director's script

This is a normal copy of the entire play, but should be interleaved with blank sheets in order to give the director space to make comments and insert his own stage directions.

Typed scripts are invariably used in **radio, television** and **films** – as the material is specially written and is not published in book form. The following points are given for the professional display of scripts. For a comparison of the basic differences, and 'Notes', see page 109.

Radio

Names of characters begin at 1 in., are typed in capitals and followed by a colon.

Dialogue begins at about $2\frac{1}{4}$ in., 3 spaces after the longest name, with a 1 in. right-hand margin.

Spacing is single or double.

Directions within the text (for interpretation by characters) should be in lower case, enclosed within brackets, and underscored.

Directions for 'effects' are inset $\frac{1}{2}$ in., typed in capitals in blocked style, enclosed within brackets, with double-line spacing before and after each direction.

Pagination. Numbers are typed centrally over the page at the top, or on the right-hand side. In the case of a serial, each episode begins at page 1.

Speeches are each numbered consecutively down the page at $\frac{1}{2}$ in., and each page is re-numbered from 1.

Page turnover should come at the end of a speech, but if this is impossible it must be at the end of a sentence, followed by spaced dots to the right-hand margin, with '(continued)' justified below.

Task 22

Typist Please send this off straight away – we might be lucky!

The Advertiser, Box 189 (FJ), The Weekly News, High Street, Reading RG8 9BB

Dear Sir, In to-day's issue of the local paper I see you are offering for sale several typewriters "as new" → [though you do not specify whether they are manual, electric or electronic.] I should be grateful if you (would) phone me at the above ~~ad~~ number so that we can arrange a mutually convenient time (for me) to see them.

Yours ffy

Task 23

Mrs. A. Freemantle of 43a Orchard Ave, Orpington Kent BR6 9UA did not complete her form correctly when she called – please send her the following letter.

Cruise No. T/182

Before we can complete arrangements for yr. holiday I should be grateful if you wd. provide us with the following information:

1. The number of yr. passport
2. Do you intend travelling from London, or will you make your own way to S'ton?
3. Do you wish to take out an insurance policy against possible cancellation of yr. booking?

As soon as this information is received we shall send you the necessary documents.

Yours ff

caps. Happi Holidays Ltd.

Assistant Manager.

10 The Entertainment World

With the ever-increasing popularity of television, and radio's constant listening public, there has naturally been a demand for more scripts, and this requires competent typists.

Each of the areas of entertainment, theatre, radio, television and films either calls on the services of a secretarial bureau specialising in this field, or has its own typing department. It is important to know the correct layout, as scripts are displayed differently in each of the four media. Whilst there are basic rules, however, each producer may have his/her own particular preference for display, so that the typist should be adaptable and follow copy and instructions for each piece of work undertaken.

The typing of plays for the theatre

Producers of plays for the theatre frequently wish to indicate their own interpretations, even of well-known and classic dramatisations, so that, although books may be obtainable, they prefer to have typescripts for themselves and their cast in order to be able to add notes or indicate cuts. With the use of word processors and other equipment in the technological office, it is often cheaper, and certainly more advantageous, to produce individually typed scripts.

There is a generally recognised layout for the typing of plays, though it may differ in detail from company to company. However, three main 'stops' are common to all: Character Stop, Dialogue Stop and Direction Stop.

General notes

1 **Character Stop** tab is at $1\frac{1}{2}$ in. from the left-hand edge of the paper; the names of the characters are typed in capitals. (If any name is particularly long, an author may require an abbreviation to be used.)
2 **Dialogue Stop** is the main margin, set 3 in. from the edge of the paper (though all names must be accommodated), with a $\frac{1}{2}$ in. right-hand margin.
3 **Direction Stop** tab is set at 4 in. with a 1 in. right-hand margin, ie directions are inset.

Note: The first page of each Act begins at the same point with a dropped heading. All other pages have a 1 in. margin at the top. All bottom margins are 1 in.

Line spacing. Single spacing is used, with double between speeches and before and after directions typed at the direction stop. An extra space may be left after the Scene directions at the beginning of each Act for clarity.

Acts and scenes

1 Dropped head for 'ACT', which is typed in capitals, with the number either in words (capitalized) or in *large* roman numerals.
2 'Scene' is typed in lower case with an initial capital, and follows the style of the Act, ie number in words (initial capital) or *small* roman numerals.
3 ACT and Scene can each be centred over the whole, or typed side by side (allowing several spaces between for clarity) either at the Dialogue Stop or at the Direction Stop.

Pagination

1 First pages of Acts are not always numbered.
2 All other pages are numbered consecutively for each separate Act.
3 Pages are numbered at the top right-hand side, $\frac{1}{2}$ in. down, with three sets of figures for quick reference, eg I–4–32 (Act I, Scene 4, page 32 of that Act).
4 In One-act plays, pages are similarly numbered, either I–2–25 or 2–25.

Scene and stage directions

1 At the beginning of each Act they are usually typed in lower case, with characters' names in capitals, at the Dialogue or Direction Stop (according to the style used for Acts and Scenes – *see* above) with $\frac{1}{2}$ in. right-hand margin.
2 At the beginning of a speech, the stage directions usually begin with a lower-case letter, and are enclosed within brackets at the Dialogue Stop.
3 Directions relating to the character *speaking* are generally enclosed within brackets.
4 Within the play, they begin at the Direction Stop, with a 1 in. right-hand margin. They are typed in lower case, the name of any character mentioned being typed in full capitals. Single spacing is used with double spacing before and after each direction.
5 Directions for characters not at the moment

Task 24

This is a letter from a London Specialist to Dr C S Bushell, whose practice is at The Red House, Ventnor, Isle of Wight PO38 2NY

Dear Dr. Bushell,

Thank you for your letter, introducing Mrs F. Gower (GOWER), of 168, Castle View Ave. Ventnor.

I have given her a thorough examination & agree (with you) that the cause of the trouble is a disc lesion (as the patient feared). I am quite certain that, in any case there is no evidence whatsoever of Carcenoma! (CARCINOMA)

She might try a period of rest in bed, at home (on boards) for 3 weeks, & if there is no improvement, let me know & I will arrange for her to go into hospital for treatment.

She has been told to contact you early next week, when she will be back in Ventnor, & I now leave her in your hands.

Yours sincerely,

Please type this table + display as indicated. The name of each ruler should take up one line only.

caps + u/s

BRITISH RULERS

House of Stuart to House of Windsor

Ruler	accession	Died	Age	Reigned years
caps → House of Stuart				
James I (VI of Scotland)	1603	1625	59	22
Charles I	1625	1649	48	24
Commonwealth + Protectorate				
Oliver Cromwell, Lord Protector	1653	1658	59	-
Richard " "	1658	1712	86	-
House of Stuart (Restored)				
Charles II	1660	1685	55	25
James II (VII of Scotland)	1685	1701	68	3
William III }	1689	1702	51	13
Mary II }		1694	33	6
Anne	1702	1714	49	12
House of Hanover				
George I	1714	1727	67	13
George II	1727	1760	77	33
" III	1760	1820	81	59
" IV	1820	1830	67	10
William IV	1830	1837	71	7
Victoria	1837	1901	81	63
House of Saxe-Coburg				
Edward VII	1901	1910	68	9
House of Windsor				
George V	1910	1936	70	25
Edward VIII	1936	1972	78	325 days
George VI	1936	1952	56	15
Elizabeth II	1952	-	-	-

Footnotes: a = abdicated b = beheaded d = deposed r = resigned

Typist: An extra column is required between "Accession" + "Died" – headed "Reign or Rule Ceased". The dates will be the same as for "Died" except: R. Cromwell 1659r James II 1688d + Edward VIII 1936a. Above the five narrow columns, please type headings vertically.

Task 25

The following four skeleton specimen letters are required for the Accounts Department. (The dots represent the information to be added at the time of sending the letter.) Sufficient space should be left between each of the letters for them to be quite clear.

Specimen skeleton Letters for Overdue Accounts

A. on approval/ May we remind you that on ... we sent you a parcel containing ... book/s on Invoice No. ... The book/s was/were sent ~~to you~~ for one month heard/ As we have not ~~received the parcel~~ from you, we assume you have the book/s decided to keep ~~it~~, and therefore we should be glad if you would send us the remittance of ...

B. We note with regret that you have not replied to our letter of ... in which we asked for a settlement of yr. a/c in respect Para- of the item/s on Invoice No. ... [It may be that our first letter went astray. We are writing you again (therefore) with the request ively/ that you send us a remittance of ... or, alternately, that you return the book/s to us. Add * as new para.

C. Our letters of ... and ... requesting a settlement of yr. a/c with us for ... on Invoice No. ... have still not been answered. [We feel there must be a very reasonable explanation ~~excuse~~ long/ for yr. silence, but, as yr. a/c is overdue, we must insist that payment is made by ...

D. We very much regret that as we have neither received the book/s sent to you on ... on Invoice No. ..., nor received the amount of ... due to us, as mentioned in our last letter of the ..., we must insist that payment be made by return of post.

If, therefore, this a/c is not settled by the ... we shall ~~be forced~~ (have no alternative but) to place the matter in the hands of our Solicitors.

* We should appreciate an early settlement of this a/c.

Typist I think you had better type this series of letters in triplicate. Mark the top copy for me, one for a/c's Dept. + one for file.

Using specimen C. will you write to Mrs. J. Davies of 21 Watermill Rd. Preston, Lancs PR2 3TU who has ignored our letters dated 3rd + 25th of last month. Invoice No B.162 39/ She owes £31.25. Payment within 7 days.

(Final letters will be signed by the Manager of the A/Cs Dept.) Type in caps

Task 72

Typist – Please set these books out as a table (ruling not necessary) with the following headings: Author – Title – Publisher – Number of pages + Reference number. Put subject headings above each section in first column. Authors to be in alphabetical order, surnames in caps, + put an asterisk on the left of the title if the book has any illustrations. (Give a key)

SUGGESTED BOOKS FOR LECTURE TOUR – SECTION II

① Natural History

Giraffes – C.A.W. Goggisberg (Arthur Barker) [96 pp] 16 colour plates (0213 76305 2)

Seals – K.M. Backhouse (Arthur Barker) [96 pp] 16 colour plates (0213 76326 5)

Flowers of Europe: a Field Guide – Oleg Polunin (O.U.P.) [704] 192 plates in colour 50 pp of line drawings (ISBN 0-19-217621-8)

Birds of Asia – John Gould + Abram Rutgers (Methuen) [322 pp] 160 full colour plates (ISBN 0 416 95400 6)

③ Sports + Hobbies

The Book of Canoeing – Dennis J. Dennis (Arthur ~~Baker~~ BARKER) [112 pp] 35 illustrations (0213 17804 4)

The Past of Pastimes – Vernon Bartlett (Chatto + Windus) Illustrated (07011 1406 1)

Techniques of Philately – L.N + M. Williams (Heinemann) [144 pp] 16 pp half tones

Underwater Swimming – Leo Zanelli (Kaye + Ward) [128 pp] 7 photos (ISBN 0 7182 0753 x)

Better Athletics – John Heaton (Kaye + Ward) [96 pp] /a Photos throughout (ISBN 0 7182 0155 8)

② Travel + Adventure

Doing England with a Giraffe – Ivan Boldizsar (Macmillan) [240 pp] (ISBN 0 333 10156 8)

Kiwi Vagabond – Errol Allison (Robert Hale) (ISBN 07091 0602 5)

This is Washington D.C – M. Sasek (W.H. Allen) illustrated throughout (ISBN 0 491 00799 x) [64 pp]

A Sight of China – Cynthia Noble (Macmillan) [192]

The Sahara is yours – Jon Stevens (Constable) [288] 17 photos (009 456230 x)

Coast of the Sun: Travels in Portugal – Henry C. James [176 pp] (Jarrolds) 31 illustrations

Task 26

FOSTER & FOSTER LIMITED

House Furnishers

Telephone
Fairlands 04567

35 Main Street,
PURLEY, Surrey,
CR2 4TJ

Settatree & Fords Co Ltd
John Street
Leeds
LS10 2HJ

Dear Sirs

Enclosed herewith our cheque for £185.50 (one hundred and ninety-five pounds fifty) in settlement of the enclosed account.

The goods we received from you were of a very high quality and are selling well, so that we shall be sending a similar order within the next fortnight and hope you will be able to deliver without any delay.

Yours faithfully

Accounts Department

WRT/jm

enc

Typist Will you please send the following letter to Foster & Foster, together with their cheque & a copy of their letter.* Note the discrepancy in the figures & point this out in the usual way.

We thank you for your letter received this morning, but undated, together with your cheque for £185.50 (one hundred & eighty-five pounds fifty). (run on) As you will see from our a/c, the amount owing to us is £195.50. [I am sending you a copy of your letter to us, from which you will see that the figures & words do not agree, & ⊙ no doubt the cheque was made out from the figures. I am returning yr. cheque & shd. be grateful if you wd. send another in replacement. o/c

Yours f.

Manager
Accounts Dept.

* This will have to be typed as the photocopier is still not working.

Task 71

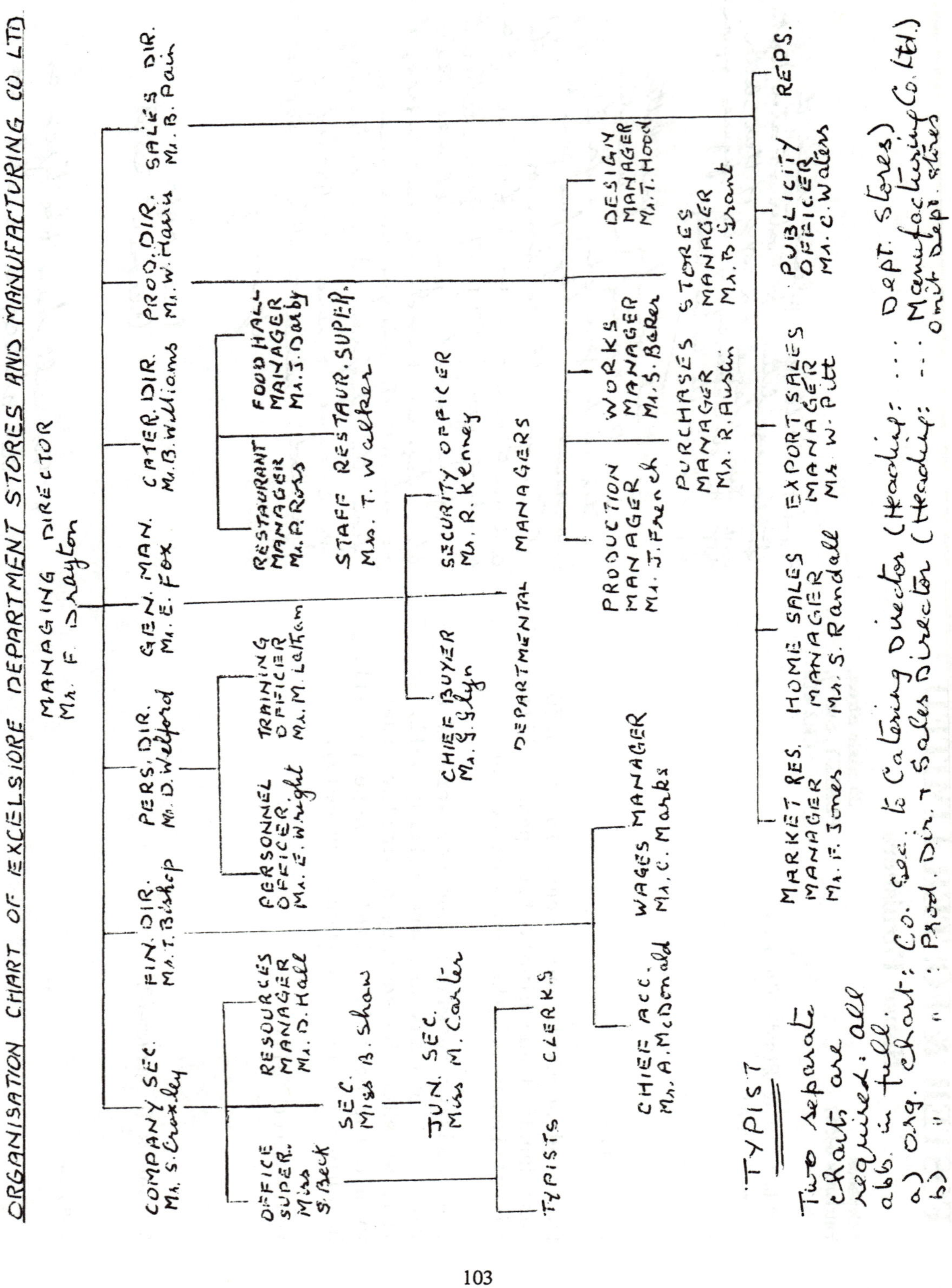
ORGANISATION CHART OF EXCELSIORE DEPARTMENT STORES AND MANUFACTURING CO LTD
MANAGING DIRECTOR Mr. F. Drayton
COMPANY SEC. Mr. S. Croxley
FIN. DIR. Mr. T. Bishop
PERS. DIR. Mr. D. Welford
GEN. MAN. Mr. E. Fox
CATER. DIR. Mr. B. Williams
PROD. DIR. Mr. W. Harris
SALES DIR. Mr. B. Pain
OFFICE SUPER. Miss S. Beck
RESOURCES MANAGER Mr. D. Hall
SEC. Miss B. Shaw
JUN. SEC. Miss M. Carter
TYPISTS
CLERKS
PERSONNEL OFFICER Mr. E. Wright
TRAINING OFFICER Mr. M. Latham
CHIEF BUYER Mr. J. Glyn
SECURITY OFFICER Mr. R. Kenney
DEPARTMENTAL MANAGERS
RESTAURANT MANAGER Mr. P. Ross
FOOD HALL MANAGER Mr. J. Darby
STAFF RESTAUR. SUPER. Mrs. T. Walker
CHIEF ACC. Mr. A. McDonald
WAGES MANAGER Mr. C. Marks
PRODUCTION MANAGER Mr. J. French
WORKS MANAGER Mr. S. Baker
DESIGN MANAGER Mr. T. Hood
PURCHASES MANAGER Mr. R. Austin
STORES MANAGER Mr. B. Grant
MARKET RES. MANAGER Mr. F. Jones
HOME SALES MANAGER Mr. S. Randall
EXPORT SALES MANAGER Mr. W. Pitt
PUBLICITY OFFICER Mr. C. Waters
REPS.
TYPIST
Two separate charts are required: all abb. in full.
a) Org. chart: Co. Sec. to Catering Director (Heading: ... Dept. Stores)
b) " " : Prod. Dir. + Sales Director (Heading: ... Manufacturing Co. Ltd.) omit Dept. stores

Task 27

Typist — Will you make me a draft, please, to see how it looks. It is to be personalised when it goes out next month.

Dear ___

Have you read any good books recently? — Yes I thought so, but have you bought any good books recently? — no? Because they are too expensive no doubt.

There are many book clubs, but they offer a very limited choice. This is where the Readers Choice Book Club is different.

Choice of Books — caps/

Once you are a member of the RCBC (keep abb.), you can build up a library with the books wh interest you. You will be entitled to choose one book every month. Here are just a few of the subjects to set you thinking: — a wide range of topics & a wide range of titles

1. Scientific works of every description
3. Nature and the world of animals
2. Sports & Athletics
1. Biographies & Autobiographies
5. Novels — classical & modern: some large print editions

When you become a member you will be sent a comprehensive list fr wh to make a selection. u/c in/

The Beauty of the Books

The books offered by the R-C-B-C will enhance yr book-case. They are beautifully bound in imitation leather with gold lettering. The variety of colours indicates the subject grouping, ie all books on gardening are in green, whilst biographies are in blue. They are uniform in size & easy to handle. coloured

Membership of the RCBC

To take advantage of our offer, you have only to fill in the enc. form & send it, together with yr cheque, & you will receive each month — your own choice of book.

It gives me great pleasure to welcome you, in advance, to the R-C-B-C. This is a wonderful offer wh I feel sure you will appreciate.

Yours s.

Task 70

The following information is required in tabular form. The left-hand column should show the grades, the right-hand column should show the totals in each grade, with details in the intervening columns. Totals in each category should be given at the foot of each column.

Confidential

PERSONNEL DEPARTMENT

No. of Employees in Each Wage Group
(Permanent Staff)

GRADE I

Men: Under 18 220
Over 18 —

Women: Under 18 25
Over 18 2

GRADE II

M. Under 18 24
Over 18 316

W. Under 18 —
Over 18 54

GRADE III

M. Under 18 3
Over 18 450

W. Over 18 96

GRADE IV

M. Over 18 320

W. " 18 72

GR. V

M. 75 W. 20

GR. VI

M. 18 W. 1

GR. VII M. 2 W. —

Totals

Grade I 247
" II 394
III 549
IV 392
V 95
VI 19
VII 2
1,698

Men

Under 18 247
Over 18 1,181

Women

Under 18 25
Over 18 245
1,698

Task 28

Typist

Mr. Richardson has asked that you type the following letter, as for signature. He wants to check with Mr. Taylor before it goes out. You can date it for tomorrow.

This is to let you know that now I have been so asked.

Mrs D Grey
The Larches
Beacon Rise
Weston
Blankshire

Your Reference

Our Reference
CV/E/4507
Date

Dear Mrs Grey

ROAD IMPROVEMENT AT BEACON RISE

When you called at this Office recently I promised to let you know as soon as I was asked by the Weston ~~Urban~~ Borough Council to advise upon terms which I can recommend to the Council, & any Government Dept concerned, (in full) for the purchase of a strip of land forming part of yr (in full) front garden, shown in pink ~~colour~~ on the attached plan & having an area of 40 sq. m.

Mr Taylor, a valuer in this office, will be in your locality on Monday next. I trust this will be convenient to you. I would like to inspect the land at about 10.30 am.

NP If you decide to appoint a surveyor to advise you in this matter & if a purchase is effected, I would be prepared to recommend the payment by the acquiring authority, as part of the terms of the settlement, of such amount in respect of professional advice as is proper & reasonable in the circumstances of the case. The Authority would also pay your proper legal costs.

Yours sincerely

L. C. Richardson
District Valuer & Valuation Officer

Task 69

Typist Details are required, in tab. form (ruled) to show County - Town - Approx. Population - Distance from London (miles + kilometres) and early closing. Please use these headings. Counties should be in alphabetical order + towns also within the counties (Each county need be typed once only)

SOUTH COAST TOWNS

Preliminary survey for Hodgson + Company

Town	County	Population (Approx.)	Distance from London Km	Miles	Early Closing
Ramsgate	Kent	40,000	119	74	Thursday
Folkestone	Kent	45,000	112	70	Wednesday
Hastings	E. Sussex	68,000	107	63	Wednesday
Dover	Kent	38 000	116	72	Wed./Sat.
Eastbourne	East Sussex	67 000	103	64	Wed.
Brighton	E. Sx	164 000	85	53	Wed./Thurs
Worthing	W. Sx	82000	93	58	Wed.
Portsmouth/Southsea	Hampshire	219,000	114	71	Wed
Southampton	"	212 000	124	77	Wed
Bournemouth	"	152000	167	104	Wed/Sat.
Weymouth	Dorset	44,000	212	132	Wednesday
Exeter	Devon	94 000	274	170	Wed/Sat
Torquay	"	54000	307	191	Wed/Sat
Plymouth	"	215 000	340	211	Thurs.
St. Austell	Cornwall	28000	389	242	Thurs/Fri
Falmouth	"	19000	430	267	Wed.
Bognor	W. Sx	32 000	105	65	Wed.

Task 29

Type the following letters with care and insert the accents neatly.

a

18th February, 19--

Mr. L. B. Brown,
23 Birchwood Grove
Coventry.
CV3 2JG

Dear Mr. Brown,

Thank you very much for your letter requesting information on sight-seeing holidays in Great Britain. We suggest the following might be of interest to you:–

1. Grand Coach Tour of England, Scotland and Wales (3 weeks).
2. Area Coach Tours (2 and 3 weeks) of the West Country, the South Coast, the Heart of England, the Lake District, Scotland, Wales and Ireland.

I am enclosing brochures giving details of the above holidays. I would point out that guests stay at only first-class hotels.

Prices, which vary with the tour chosen, can be obtained from the tariffs enclosed with the brochures.

We do, of course, arrange for all travel to and from your destination, either by train or air, as required.

Should you wish any further information to help you plan your holiday, please do not hesitate to contact us.

Yours sincerely,
Encs.

b

Monsieur Fréderic Lemonnier,
27 rue de Londres,
75009 Paris, Cédex,
France.

Brighton le 18 février 19 - -

Monsieur,

Nous vous remercions de votre lettre par laquelle vous nous demandez des renseignements au sujet de vos vacances en Grande Bretagne. Les propositions suivantes pourraient vous convenir:

1. Grand circuit en autocar (Angleterre, Ecosse, Pays de Galles) de 3 semaines
2. Circuits régionaux en autocar (2 ou 3 semaines) de la région de l'ouest, de la côte sud, du centre du pays, de la région des lacs, ou encore de l'Ecosse, du Pays de Galles et de l'Irlande.

Nous vous adressons ci-joint des brochures donnant tous détails sur ces circuits. Il vous intéressera de savoir que les hôtels séléctionnés sont tous de première catégorie.

Nos prix, qui varient selon le voyage choisi, sont indiqués dans le tarif également ci-joint.

Il va sans dire que nous pouvons organiser votre voyage aller et retour à partir de Paris, en train ou en avion, selon votre choix.

En restant à votre disposition pour tous renseignements complémentaires, nous vous prions de croire, Monsieur, à l'expression de nos sentiments les plus distingués.

P.J.

c

18. Februar 19--

Herrn
Gernot Schmidt,
Friedberger Strasse 22,
6200 Wiesbaden,
West Germany.

Sehr geehrter Herr Schmidt,

Wir bestätigen dankend den Erhalt Ihres Schreibens, worin Sie uns um Auskunft über Reisen in Grossbritannien bitten. Wir machen folgende Vorschläge, die Sie interessieren könnten:

1. Gross Rundreise mit Reiseautobus durch England, Schottland und Wales (3 Wochen)
2. Reisen (2 oder 3 Wochen) mit Reiseautobus durch Westengland, die Südküste, Mittelengland, Seengebiet, Schottland, Wales, Irland.

Beiliegend senden wir Ihnen Broschüren mit allen Einzelheiten über die obigen Reisen. Wir weisen darauf hin, dass die Reisenden nur in erstklassigen Hotels untergebracht werden.

Die Preise richten sich nach der gewählten Rundreise, genaue Einzelheiten bitten wir Sie den beiliegenden Broschüren zu entnehmen.

Die Buchungen für Hin- und Rückreise nach dem von Ihnen gewählten Bestimmungsort, können wir für Sie erledigen, je nach Wunsch entweder mit der Bahn oder dem Flugzeug.

Wir sind Ihnen gern behilflich bei der Zusammenstellung und Planung Ihrer Reise, und würden uns freuen diesbezüglich wieder von Ihnen zu hören.

Mit freundlichen Grüssen,

Anl.

Task 68

EXPORT AND IMPORT FIGURES FOR
DOMESTIC ELECTRICAL APPLIANCES

(January to April 19..* and 19..Ŧ)

Appliances		Exports (£000's)		Imports (£000's)	
		Four months ended		Four months ended	
	April 19..*	April 19..*	April 19Ŧ	April 19--*	April 19--Ŧ
Refrigerators and parts	280	1,100	1,424	1,400	644
Washing machines all types	240	1,188	2,489 }	170	382
Washing machine parts	243	1,210	1,469 }		
Dishwashers	34	133	133		
Fans	63	337	504 }		
Floor polishers	17	101	151 }		
Food mixers	49	264	231 }	1,086	579
Vacuum cleaners	170	1,187	1,544 }		
Clocks, etc.	335	1,667	1,383 }		
Cookers	47	194	293 }		
Cooking appliances and parts	110	390	505 }		
Heaters, Space	42	374	318 }	569	465
Heaters, Water	30	124	113 }		
Irons, Electric	57	239	265 }		
Heaters and parts (others)	171	691	734 }	489	489
Total, Domestic appliances	1,888	9,199	11,556	3,714	2,559

[Note: * = Last April   Ŧ = Previous april]

TYPIST a) Export figures are required as above. Please make a tabular statement + rule, putting appliances in alphabetical order – "parts" to follow item.

b) Memo from Tony Jacobs, Electrical Manager, to B. Pain, Sales Manager, suggesting that in future figs. be given separately for sales of appliances + "other parts" in all cases. a truer comparison of articles exported would emerge. Take an extra copy of both for Mr. T. Wood for information. (I fear the photocopier is still not working!)

Task 30

Mr. and Mrs. J. F. May

request the pleasure of the company of

Miss Betty Rees

at the marriage of their daughter

MARGARET JEAN

to

MR. BERNARD BRISTOW

at

St. Andrew's Church, Dundee

on Saturday, 20th June, 19..

at 12 noon

Kinloch,
Victoria Avenue,
Dundee, Scotland.

R.S.V.P.

Miss Brown

Please display the following reply to the above invitation. Home address: Redmayes, Tudor Drive, Chester, Cheshire CH4 7LB

Miss Betty Rees regrets that, as she will be spending the next six months in Africa, she is unable to accept the kind invitation of Mr & Mrs J.F. May to the marriage of their daughter, Margaret Jean, to Mr Bernard Bristow at St. Andrew's Church, Dundee on Saturday, 20 June, 19..

Task 31

Mr. and Mrs. J. B. Brett

request the pleasure of the company of

Miss Betty Rees

at a Cocktail Party

to celebrate their Silver Wedding

at

The Clifton Hall Hotel, Torquay

on Saturday, 22nd June 19--

from 6 p.m.

The Heights,
Torbay Avenue,
Torquay, Devon.

R.S.V.P.

Miss Brown

Please accept the invitation to Mr & Mrs Brett's Silver wedding on my behalf.

Task 66

TRAINING RECORDS – APTITUDES

DEPT

NAMES	Dates	Expertise	Distribution	Service to Customers	Credit Procedures	Till Procedures	Admin	Health + Safety at Work	FINAL ASSESSMENT
	(8)	(6)	(3)	(7)	(2)	(1)	(4)	(5)	(9)
SMITH B									
BROWN J									
JENKINS S									
KENNEY A									
TRUMAN S									
BARLOW C									
GRIFFITHS O									

TYPIST

(1) Names in alph. order
(2) Add: T. Green + F. Andrews
(3) Change order of cols. as indicated

Task 67

SHARE INDICES – A SELECTION

FRIDAY 12 MAY 19--

EQUITY GROUPS AND SUB-SECTIONS Figures in parentheses show number of stocks per section		INDEX No.	DAY'S CHANGE %	EST. EARNINGS YIELD % (MAX)	GROSS DIV. YIELD % (ACT AT 30%)	EST. P/E RATIO (NET)
1	CAPITAL GOODS (208)	454.06	+0.2	8.70	3.82	14.72
2	Building Materials (23)	416.42	-0.1	10.02	4.75	12.37
4	Electricals (33)	1716.87	+0.4	7.03	2.04	18.38
6	Mechanical Engineering (64)	211.02	-0.3	11.51	5.48	10.85
		414.67	+0.4	10.31	4.42	11.81
21	CONSUMER GROUP (201)	324.33	-0.2	13.80	5.89	8.51
25	Food Manufacturing (21)	521.39	-0.4	7.52	4.64	17.66
29	Leisure (24)					
35	Textiles (22)	201.33	-0.9	12.41	5.63	9.30
41	OTHER GROUPS (79)	334.35	-0.1	8.48	4.92	14.81
44	Office Equipment (6)	100.85	-0.8	8.74	5.58	14.72
45	Shipping + Transport (14)	646.05	-0.1	9.03	6.20	14.47

TYPIST

(1) Oblique headings in l.c. with initial caps. (ACT in caps)
(2) All abb. to be retained

Task 32

Memo

To; Mr S. Stanley. Design Dept:

From: Publicity Officer.

Thank you for letting me have the draft copy of the new catalogue so promptly. This is a great improvement on the last one.

You will see that I have made several pencilled suggestions (in the margins), Perhaps you would like to consider these, & then come along & discuss them with me.

Could you manage tomorrow, at 1500 hrs?

Task 33

Typist: Memo to go to all Directors from Office Supervisor Ref. GA/121/A

In order to streamline the services of the Gen. Office & as a result of our meeting last week I wd make the follg points:

1. Work will be distributed on a rota system
2. Typists shd be prepared to work in any of the typing areas (/ any dept)
   a) Gen Office
   ~~d~~ b) Works Office
   c) Marketing Office
   ~~b~~ d) Accounts Office

4. ~~3~~. Shd any Dir. have work which is likely to continue over a period of time, then he may wish one typist to be responsible throughout.

3 ~~4~~. Shd any Dir. wish one particular typist to be attached to him over a short period, this will be arranged.

Typist: Heading: Services of the Gen. Office (Caps)

in the form of a 'family tree', when, ideally, levels of functions or items for comparison should be placed side by side, but if this is not possible, a vertical line with its respective branches may be extended into a clear space below. With a complicated chart, it may be wise to have a 'trial run'.

Bar Charts and Pie Charts – *see* page 127

Tabular tasks

Read the instructions carefully before beginning each piece of work.

Task 65

SUMMARY OF STATE OF CONTRACTS

Types ordered	under contracts E.4147	E.5260	Total ordered by type	In process of manufacture	In assembly	Under test	In transit	Balance to be manufactured	Arrived	Installed at site (2nd figure indicates planned total to be installed) A	B	C
4041	18	18	36	11	4	2	2	17	–	0/12	0/10	0/14
4042	16	12	28	9	3	2	1	13	1	0/8	1/10	0/10
1117	42	28	70	38	16	5	8	3	6	2/23	2/23	2/24
1119	30	6	36	14	6	3	12	1	8	0/6	4/15	4/15
1120	24	24	48	10	17	6	15	0	12	4/14	8/16	0/18
1121	28	32	60	22	14	8	13	3	6	0/15	2/22	4/23
1027	144	–	144	63	28	17	26	10	19	6/44	6/50	7/50
992	12	3	15	–	2	2	11	–	8	3/3	3/6	2/6

Typist One copy please. When photocopier is repaired copies to Mr Baker for information; to Mr Shaw for attention. – attach a note to this copy to remind you.

Postcards

Task 34

Typist Memo to go to Mr. S. Freeman, Kent Area Rep.
fr. Mr. J. Randell, Sales Manager.

We have rec. a letter fr. a Mr. Philip Webster who is opening a new branch of the Guardem Assurance plc in yr district. [He will be needing office equip. & stationery & has asked us to give him quotations. I have written him (OE/S/3) today enclosing a copy of our catalogue, & informing him that you will call to see him]. You can contact him at the branch in Bootle St., telephone: 01-629 4444.
This could mean a large order so I am relying on you to make the necessary arrangements to see Mr. W. with our full range of catalogues without delay.
[Please report on this visit immediately. (within the next 3 days)

Task 35

Typist This memo is to be photocopied for all Departmental Heads
From General Manager. Heading: FLEXITIME

As a result of the Board meeting held yesterday, it has been decided th. f a trial period of one month, those wishing to work flexihours may do so. The hours worked will be remain as at present, & a full complement of staff will be expected to be on duty during the main busy periods of the day. These are:

Core times 1000 hrs to 1200 hrs
1400 . 1600 (CORE)

Before management can finalise details Department Heads should discuss the new proposal with each member of the staff to ascertain how many wish to take advantage of the flexiworking hours. (no. of) (members of staff)

9 Tabulation

Advanced and difficult tabulation needs very careful planning and preparation, especially with undisplayed manuscripts. A few extra minutes spent checking figures at the beginning will often avoid the necessity of retyping a piece of work (or wasting precious time in an examination). Special points to note:

1 Correct size of paper should be used to make statements clear and look important.
2 Statement should be centrally placed with equal margins.
3 Except in a first descriptive column, it is usual for headings in boxes to be in lower case with initial caps only (no underscore) and in single spacing.
4 Column headings should be centred within their boxes.
5 Footnotes should be centred or blocked under the tabular statement, two or three spaces below the bottom horizontal line.

Tabulation within continuous matter

This should be centred, or blocked at the left-hand margin, according to the style used in the continuous matter, and should appear complete on any one page.

Formation of tabular statements

Careful planning is required, possibly with the use of a diagram, lightly pencilled marks and a ruler. If complex, it may be necessary to draft the statement before typing.

Vertical headings

These are used when columns are too narrow to accommodate the headings horizontally. Consistency must be maintained, the only exception being that the first column, usually the widest, may take a horizontal heading whilst the remainder are vertical. Where possible, columns should all be the same width, but the requirements of the statement itself, and a generally pleasing appearance must be considered.

When making calculations in order to work out the number of line spaces to be left for the vertical headings, it is important to remember the ratio of 6 lines down the page (1 in.) being equivalent to 12 letter spaces in elite (and 10 in pica) when actually typing the headings.

Oblique headings

These are a variation on vertical headings; they are more easily read, but take up a little more space.

Planning is the same as for vertical headings, except that space for an extra column must be allowed for on the right to accommodate the last oblique heading. Typing of the statement should proceed and be completed up to the point of inserting the headings.

The outside ruling and vertical lines for the columns having been drawn from the base of the statement to the base line of the headings, the oblique lines for the headings should then be lightly pencilled in. This is done, first, by marking a dot, in pencil along the top line, immediately above its corresponding vertical line, and then by ruling from the base of the first column to the dot on the top line of the second column, and so on to the end, finishing with an overhang (one column width beyond the last column of figures).

To assist in typing the headings, a light horizontal line is pencilled in to indicate where each of the headings will begin (one space above the base line of the headings). The paper is inserted into the machine so that the alignment scale runs along the oblique lines already marked in. The headings should be centred between the parallel lines, and typing begins at the line as indicated.

When oblique headings are unequal, the above straightforward method cannot be used. It is important that the lines should all be at the *same angle*, and the easiest method is to 'estimate' the first oblique line, and then, with a ruler, slide it along and rule the subsequent oblique lines. The angle for the first oblique line would be about 30° from the perpendicular (if the line from the first vertical column were extended).

Organization charts

As explained in the section on Display (page 83), these show the level of responsibility and the relationship between these levels. Some charts are planned

Postcards

Task 36

From: Watson Bros. Commercial Rd. Sheffield S10 2SX

To : Atkinson Co. Ltd. Richmond St. Newcastle on Tyne NE1 5AH

We thank you for your letter, ref. AWL/WS/S/123 which was received today.

The goods required are not in stock, but a new consignment is expected within the next few days. On receipt of goods your order will be executed without delay.

Task 37

From: The Westlake China Co, Quarry Rd, Stone Cross, Stafford, ST18 2MA
Tel: 0785-92130 Ref Ha/107/SCS

To: Teacups, Old Square, Warwick, CV34 9BD

The information requested on our special "Festival" blue & white floral tableware is as follows:

Tea cup & saucer		£4.95
Plates for £2.50		
Milk jug (small)		£5.30
" " (large)		£5.95
Sugar bowl with lid		6.50
Tea pots	from	4.00

coffee sets & dinner services are also available

Task 38

From: Collins & Frencham Co., Ltd, Station St. Nottingham NG2 3AA

To: Mrs. Waterhouse, 29, Queen's Rd. Thirlsmere St. Leicester LE2 4PQ /G

We thank you for your order, No. B/194, & have pleasure in informing you that all items will be despatched to you within the next few days.

Ref. CF/N/B/194

BORDERS AND MENUS

o',

/_ox

0ox/

0."

%+%+%+%+%+%+%+%+%+%+%+%+%

()%()%()%()%()%()%()%()

MENU

Hûitres Natives
ou
Hors d'oeuvre Variés

—

Tortue Claire et Liée

—

Saumon d'Ecosse. Sauce Mousseline
Salade de Concombres

—

Pommes Nature
Blanchailles
Vol au Vent Toulousaine

—

Sorbet au Kummel

—

Baron d'Agneau. Sauce Menthe
Haricots Verts. Pommes Nouvelles
Asperges en Branches au Beurre

—

Fondu
Pêches Melba
Petits Fours

—

Dessert

Café

Telephone messages

Type telephone messages, with suitable display, from the given information.

Task 39

Mrs. Flemming phoned Mr. Croad to say her TV set had gone wrong again. She will not deal with anyone else. She wants to speak personally to him as soon as he comes in. Her number is 23467.

Task 40

Mr. Fielder phoned Mr. Turner to confirm the booking of 2 seats on the Lisbon plane leaving tomorrow at 1315 hrs. They are in place of ones originally booked for Sunday, & changed yesterday. If there is any query to phone Mr. Fielder – 01-072 2710.

Task 41

Mr. George phoned Mr. Wood. The 3 new typewriters are due in any day. The 2 second-hand ones are ready. Should these be delivered immediately or await arrival of new ones? His Tel. No. is 975 79210.

Composition of correspondence

Task 42

POSTCARD to Morrels Plc, Clover Parade, Swindon, SN2 2AA, from Watson Bros, Commercial Rd, Sheffield, S10 2SX. Order WS/S/125 rec. today. Goods not in stock. Consignment expected next few days. Will despatch without delay.

Task 43

MEMO from Mrs. F. Walker, Canteen Supervisor, in reply to Memo from Gen. Manager (see P. 53). Accept invitation – what time? Agree to para. on supervisor's office. Worried about Staff Room. Appears inadequate.

Task 44

LETTER to Mrs. P. Truman, Happiholidays, 289 High St, Orpington, Kent, BR6 1NS, from Miss L. Marsh, Park Mead School, Weston Rd. Orpington. Thank for phone call & help with school trip to France. Decided on Tour FR/P/51 to Paris. Request cost of extra trips: a) Tour PM/9 – Tour of Louvre b) PB/4 Boat trip on Seine c) PV/21 Day trip to Versailles.

(4) INSIDE 1: (Heading) HARDY ANNUALS

Larkspur These are the "hardy annual" relations of the stately delphinium. Blue spire 2½–3 ft.

Sweet Sultan Mixed colours. 2 ft. Large whorl-like flowers of silky texture in bloom all summer.

Nigella (Love-in-a-Mist) Mixed colours. 1½ ft. Dainty flowers particularly useful for cutting.

---

(5) INSIDE 2: (Heading) HARDY PERENNIALS

Aquilegia Mixed colours. 2 ft. Long spurred hybrids. Bloom in spring.

Coreopsis Giant Grandiflora Mayfield. 3½ ft. "Golden Marguerite" a profusion of starry flowers with broad petals, one of the best flowers for cutting.

Carnations 1½ ft. Crimson, Salmon, Scarlet. Giant Chabaud. Plants are thick-set and bushy, bearing double blossoms.

---

(6) INSIDE 3: (Heading) SHRUBS

Senecio A rare low growing shrub for sunny position or maritime districts. Very attractive silvery-grey leaves, compact.

Veronica The Veronicas are a wonderful family of evergreen shrubs, varying considerably in form and habit, and flowering profusely during the summer and autumn.

Cotoneaster Horizontalis A very attractive genera of shrubs which will thrive under almost any conditions. An evergreen with flowers and bright red berries in winter.

7 Literary Work (General and Poetry)

General Good quality A4 paper should be used.

Spacing

a Main work double (treble if draft for correction).
b Quotations and poetry single spacing, enclosed within quotation marks. Usually inset if more than one line.

Margins

a Left is usually $1\frac{1}{2}$ in. (extra $\frac{1}{2}$ in. is left as a stitching margin). Right is $\frac{1}{2}$ in. to 1 in.
b Top and bottom 1 in. except for first page of each chapter.
c First page of each chapter has a 'Dropped Head' (2 in. to 3 in. down).

Headings

a Chapter, with dropped head, in large roman numerals, arabic numerals or all in words, centred over body of work or blocked.
b Heading in capitals and three spaces below chapter.

Pagination

a No number is given on the chapter page.
b Second and subsequent pages are numbered consecutively throughout the piece of work in arabic numerals. Type the number four spaces from the top, then turn down three line spaces to the first line of type, thus leaving one clear inch at the top of the page.
c Introduction or preface is numbered in small roman numerals.

Points to watch

a Each page (except those with chapter headings) should begin at the same point.
b Avoid ending a page with the first line of a paragraph, or beginning a page with the last line of a paragraph.
c Never hyphenate the last word of a paragraph, or at the end of a page.
d Numbers are generally written out (*see* page 25).

Footnotes

a Type a line across the page (usually margin to margin) two spaces down from the text, and begin the footnotes two spaces down again. An inch must be left at the end of the page, after the last footnote.
b Type in single spacing, with double between each separate footnote.
c Margins are often $\frac{1}{2}$ in. wider than the rest of the work (i.e. footnotes are inset).
d Reference marks are used in the following order: asterisk, dagger, double dagger, (if there are more than three, then numbers would be used).
e A reference mark is typed *immediately* after the word in the text, as a superior character, but has *one* space between it and the first word in the footnote.
f Footnotes *must* appear at the foot of the same page on which the reference is given.

They should always be at the foot of the page, even if the text occupies only part of that page.
g Footnotes in work to be sent to a printer, should be inserted immediately after the line containing the reference, with a line above and below, or grouped together at the end, numbered consecutively throughout.

Italics

Underscoring indicates to the printer that the word/s so marked should be printed in italics.

Proof reading

Whilst careful checking of all work is part of the typist's art, a more accurate end-product will result if one typist reads and another checks the proofs or original work. Errors cost money and cause delays.

Poetry

1. Type in single spacing with double or treble spacing between verses.

2. The poem should be centred, the longest line usually being taken as the criterion when calculating margins.

3. Each line begins with a capital letter.

4. The title is centred over the poem, three spaces above the first line.

5. The poet's name usually finishes at the same point as the longest line of the poem, or in line with the right-hand margin; two spaces down from the last line, preceded by a dash, and either underscored or in capitals.

Task 64

Typist. Please type the following as a 6-page leaflet on one sheet of A4. Be sure you put the information on the correct pages. 1½ inches to be left between the name of each plant and the details, for inclusion of a picture. Display attractively using capitals where required. Plants alphabetically on each page. Where applicable, give names of variety; height and colour before other general details.

① FRONT: Seadowne Nurseries, Sompting, Sussex.

Extracts from General Catalogue. (Bottom) Expert always ready to give help and guidance.

---

② BACK: All year round colour collection of rock plants and shrubs
The Collection (18 plants) carriage paid. Special Offer. No. T/130
12/~~£3~~.75. Send now for this Special Offer and for further details of our plants in our General Catalogue.

(Tear off slip) - - - - - - - - - - - - - - - - - -

Seadowne Nurseries, Sompting, Sussex. Please send:

*Special offer No. T/130 ☐

for which I enclose cheque/Postal Order for £

*General Catalogue ☐

*Tick in box as appropriate.

Name ________ Address ______________________

Block Letters Please

---

③ OUTSIDE CENTRE: (Centred heading) ROCK PLANTS

Antennaria (leave space under of 1½") Dioica rosea. 2 in. Pretty little carpeter with silvery leaves. Fluffy pink flowers.

Campanulas (Bell Flower) A very brilliant and extremely useful group of plants which flower in mid-summer. Carpatica. Blue open upturned flowers. 9-12 in.

Dimorphotheca Barbarae. The large, mauve-pink daisy-like flowers give a continuous display in the garden from May onwards. 12-18 in.

(continued)

6. 'Toothing' – or indenting:

a Blank verse, or when successive lines rhyme – no indent.

b Alternate lines rhyming – indent two or three for second, fourth, sixth lines.

c Rhyming lines generally begin at the same point.

d If a line is too long, 'hook-in' (bring remaining words to the next line, to finish flush with the preceding line).

In some poetry, a normal hanging paragraph is used in place of the hook-in.

e If lines are very uneven, discretion must be used to maintain balance, hook-in if necessary.

f A *very* short line is centred.

g A chorus begins further to the right than the rest of the verse.

Task 45

Display as a Contents page.

CONTENTS

	Page
Preface	ix
Introduction	xi

PART I

Design and Construction

CHAPTER I

Plain and Ball Bearings Compared	1

The cage – Plain and ball thrust bearings – Rolling friction – Weisbach's tests – Factors to be considered

CHAPTER II

Ball Bearing Design	8

Stribeck's law – Race track design – Pressure areas and normal stresses – Carrying capacity – Goodman's formula – Factors governing carrying capacity

CHAPTER III

Developments in Ball Bearings	18

Self-aligning type – Heathcote and Palmgren's research – Thrust load – Fatigue – Ideal specific load – Double row self-aligning ball bearing Radial load – Life of bearings – Application of formulae – Combined radial and thrust loads – Single row radial bearings – Thrust load – Influence of fatigue – Commercial test for ball bearings

Uncorrected proofs

The following two passages need careful proof reading before being retyped correctly. Spelling, spacing and printing errors are included in the forty errors made in each.

Task 46

I glacned at my aneroid. We were almost at eleven thousand feet and still rising. The air wsa now very chill. My anxiety grwe. Suppose her hands became num withthe cold ? Supose she lost her will to hold on?

Another looka tmy companion and i knew that we could not waite for the ballon to tyre. Their she hung, alimp figure hanging grimly onto life, but her Face was deathly white, her lips bleu with cold, here yes wide poen and starring with supressed fear. I had toact *now*. There was only one thing to do . Somehow I would have to take her down w ith me. We would have to entrust ourselves toa single parachute. was no alter native. She could not hold on much I knew that it would be a terrible risk, but there longer, and we had touse he rremaining strength whil it it lasted.

"Louie, your'e very plucky," I called out, try ing to encourage her – trying to give her heart forth e frightning and difficult task a head. "Don't worry, I wont leave you. I'v made up my mind – you're coming down on my para chute."

– *When the Chute Went Up*
Dolly Shepherd

Task 47

The war broek out on 4 th August 1914 and woman from all wa lks of life flocked to joine the groups of voluntry organisations whcih sudenly spragn up.

On 8th August Elizabeth and Joan jioned the Women's Emergency Corps where they were given intensive traning, including Emergency First Aid, signaling (morse and semephone) and drilling by a Grenadeir Guardsman. The WEC becam a hightly organised, proficient and disciplined Corpse, readyto undertake anything, and it was no t long before it became known asthe Women's Volunteer Reserve , with it's own women officers.When it's members first paraded in public in kaki uniforms (which they had to buy themselves) they were criticised and sneeded at: Whoever heard of women soldiers!"

In 1917 the War Office asked Mrs. (later Dame) Helne Gwynne-Vaughn to for mthe Women's Auxiliary Army Corps (WAAC) , andso was borne th first of the Womens Services– the for runner of the ATS of today

– *Women to the fore*

Task 63

Typist Please type the following advertisements as attractively as possible, being guided by the display indicated. They are to go into next months magazine.

a)

RENT - A - CAR

All makes of cars available

Day, week or period → Special rates for long-term hire

(please justify)

Rates of hire include comprehensive insurance, AA + RAC membership. Arrangements made for cars to be hired at any point in the U.K.] in full

Apply to

Rent-a-Car Hire Service

Seymour Street

London W1H 5AB

---

b)

ANTIQUES

(please justify)

SHEPHERDS OF CRAWLEY

Antiques Bought

Furniture, Jewellery④, Porcelain①, Clocks③, Glass②

Gold, Silver, Bronzes, Copper, Pewter

uc/ Coins, weapons, oils

Valuations given free

Write to

J. M. Shepherd

207 High St.

Crawley, Surrey

RH12 2AB

Caps How To Be A Producer
by
C. N. G. Matthews
Caps Taped Talks and Discussions

Too many people look upon a tape
recorder only as a clever device which
not only will enable them to record and replay some
music. Excellent though it is for this
purpose, it is equally valuable for dramatics
but for serious discussions and debates. Some of
and radio the BBC television programmes consisting
of just a few people arguing and/or ans-
finest/ wering questions are among the best and
most popular entertainments of today.
Why not produce your own entertainment? NP
NP/ Recording a discussion is easier than recor-
reasonably/ ding an orchestra, but for a professional
result you must pay a great deal of att-
ention to microphone position and the
would be well advised to grouping of your cast. You should start
by recording a single speaker and then to
gain practice at getting dialogues onto tape
before attempting a full-scale debate.
NP/ ~~Another speaker~~ gives you the kind of prac-
tice in microphone technique and editing
that you could never hope to gain by rec-
ording your own voice. You know what
you are going to say, your first problem

A speaker other than yourself

but another speaker can always spring
surprises on you.

(continued)

Task 62

Joan I am giving a cookery demonstration next week & shall want to distribute the following as a 4-page booklet. Would you please type me a copy - & stencil later. Display each page clearly to the best advantage.

FRONT COVER

COOKERY DEMONSTRATION

Exciting Ideas with Cornflour

to be given at The Thorncliffe Rooms, Manchester on Tuesday (insert date) at 2.30 pm.// at foot of page display within a box 3 x 9 cm: Cooking w cornflour (in caps) - 50 delicious recipes f sauces, casseroles, desserts & baking

INSIDE LEFT

Cauliflower Palermo [PALERMO]

1 Cauliflower; 1oz. butter; 1oz cornflour; 3/4 pt. tomato juice; squeeze of lemon juice; 1 teasp. Worcester sauce, pepper & salt, 2oz. grated cheese, 1 small tin shrimps

Method — Cook the cauliflower carefully to retain its shape. Drain & place on a large serving dish & keep hot. Make a sauce with the butter, cornflour & tomato juice. Add the lemon juice, Worcester sauce & seasoning to taste. Stir in half the grated cheese & the drained shrimps. Pour carefully over the cauliflower & sprinkle with the rest of the grated cheese. Brown under the grill. Serve hot

INSIDE RIGHT

Pineapple Sundae

1 pkt. pineapple flavoured cornflour; 1oz. sugar; 3/4 pt. milk; 8oz. tinned pineapple pieces; 12 oz. chopped marshmallows; whipped cream; angelica.

Method: Mix the cornflour & sugar with a little of the cold milk & put the rest of the milk on to heat. When almost boiling, combine with mixed cornflour & cook for 1 min., stirring constantly. Remove from the heat & stir in pineapple (save a few pieces for decoration) & its syrup, & the marshmallows (stirring until dissolved). Leave to cool, then put into tall glasses, layered with / cream. Decorate with pineapple, angelica & whipped cream. (the marshmallows are)

whipped /

BACK COVER

Apricot Almond Tart

almond pastry: 5 tablesps. Mazola corn oil; 2½ tablesps iced water; 7oz. plain flour; 1oz. chopped, blanched almonds; ¼ level teasp. salt; level; little water; 4oz. sugar (for fresh apricots); blanched almonds & cherries for decoration; 2 level teasps. cornflour

Filling — 1lb fresh or ~~canned~~ tinned ~~apr~~ apricots;

To make pastry: Blend corn oil & water well together with a fork. Gradually add the flour & salt sifted together, & work in chopped almonds. Mix with a fork / to make a rollable dough, adding more flour if required. Roll out between 2 sheets of greaseproof paper & use it to line a flat plate. Prick well, & bake blind in a hot oven, 420°F, Mark 6, for 20 mins.

or palette knife /

Filling: Make a syrup of water & sugar if using fresh apricots, or bring fruit syrup left in tin to ¼ pt. with water. Arrange apricots in baked pastry case, decorate with glacé cherries & blanched almonds. Heat remaining syrup & mix cornflour smoothly with cold water, add to syrup & boil for 2-3 mins, stirring constantly. When cool, pour over apricots.

in starting this kind of work

→ will be finding a suitable speaker – no doubt you would have little difficulty in finding somebody who would read aloud

out of a book just to oblige you

but this is not at all suitable. Your speaker must enter into the spirit of the work he is doing for its own sake, otherwise you can never hope to achieve a convincing recording.

Caps

Choosing a Speaker.

Among your family and

~~Within your circle of~~ friends you will find all the speakers you need, but there are certain types which will give you the best results. One is the born performer, the person who is enthusiastic over the works of Shakespeare or Dickens – he is perhaps your best first choice – give him the opportunity + the right kind of help in production and he will work like a demon to achieve perfection.

or some other great writer

u.c.

Another good prospect is the person who has a mission. The ~~subject does not matter~~, but the enthusiasm is essential. This is another type who will struggle tirelessly towards perfection // A less satisfying, but more amusing subject, is the ~~would be~~ orator: amateur.

~~The~~ object is immaterial

pompous self-styled

Add A or

Task 61(b)

TYPIST One copy of this flow chart please – head up, in caps. "To Buy or not to buy? – That is the question"

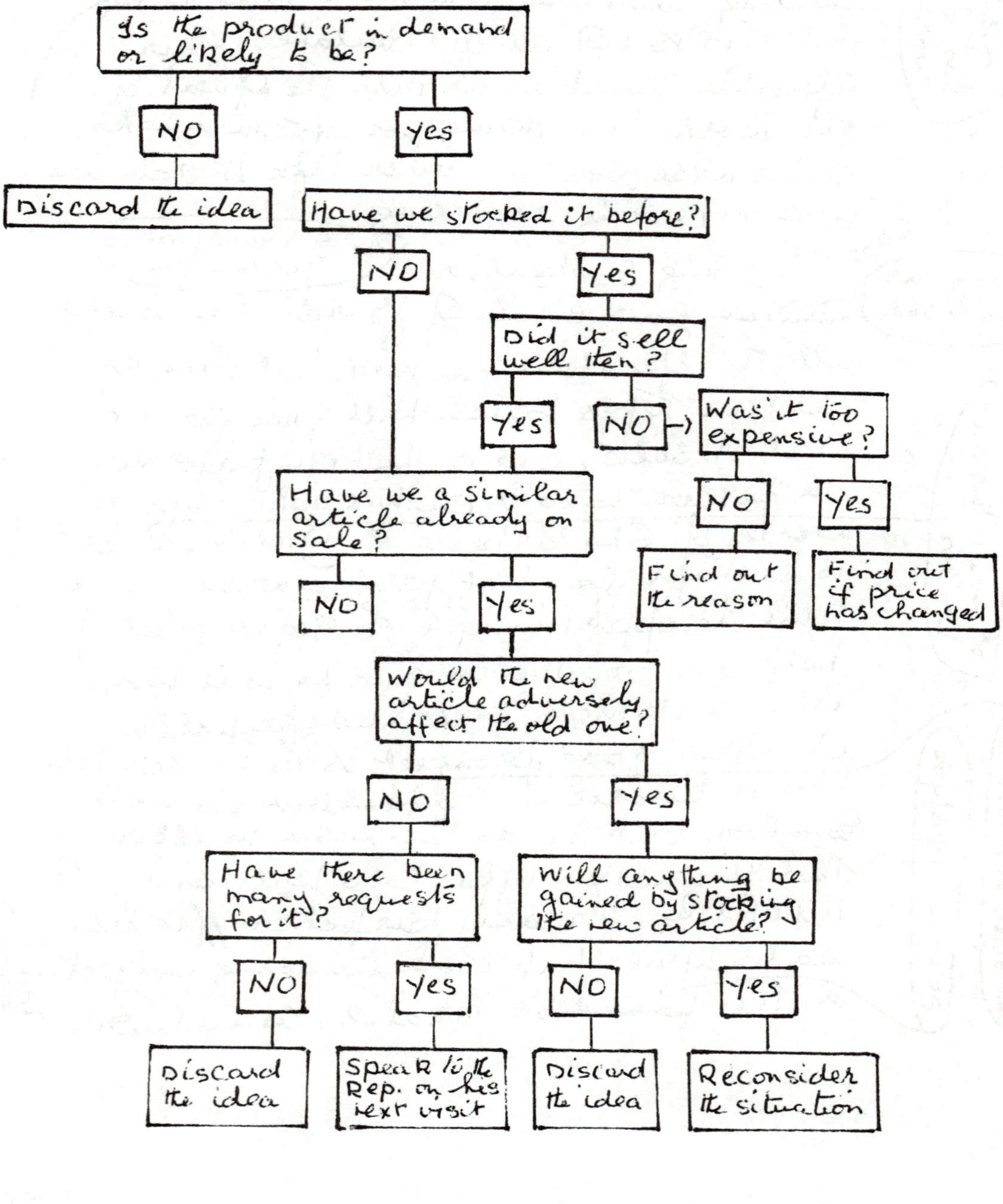

politicians and the members of some minor political parties are excellent examples. They seem to have learned a collection of set phrases and peculiar meth metaphors which they apply to any occasion. Listen to a recorded Speech l.c. of this type and you will ~~realise~~ appreciate that a little editing, including the ~~changing~~ of words, and the introduction of sound effects, will make it into a first-class Comedy l.c. monologue - but it is advisable not to try this kind of editing on a near relative!

(by heart) (transposition)

"A" when you show him how the tape recorder can help him develop better ways of putting over his point of view.

Typist
Please display heading & will you add a footnote on the first page: Taken from the book "Tape Recording" published by Pitman

Task 61(a)

<u>Typist</u> One copy please of this Organisation Chart of Directors & their fields of Responsibility - Give heading to chart.

- CHAIRMAN and MANAGING DIRECTOR — Mr F. Drayton
  - NON-EXECUTIVE DIRECTORS (2)
  - FINANCIAL DIRECTOR — Mr T. Bishop
    - Accounts
    - Costing
    - Control of cash
    - Credit control
    - Wages
  - COMPANY SECRETARY — Mr S. Croxley
    - Legal matters
    - Insurance
    - Contracts
    - Administration
    - Sec. & clerical services
    - Resources Centre
  - PERSONNEL DIRECTOR — Mr D. Welford
    - Recruiting of staff
    - Training
    - Welfare/Recreation
    - Holiday Rotas
    - Pensions
    - Fire Precautions
  - GENERAL MANAGER — Mr E. Fox
    - Departmental store (overall control)
    - Staff (overall control in store)
    - Buyers
    - Promotions/sales
    - Security
  - CATERING DIRECTOR — Mr T. Harris
    - Restaurant
    - Staff restaurant
    - Food Hall
    - Purchases
    - Hygiene
  - PRODUCTION DIRECTOR — Mr J. Williams
    - Production
    - Works management
    - Maintenance
    - Stores & stock control
    - Purchases
    - Research & Design
  - SALES DIRECTOR — Mr B. Pain
    - Market Research (4)
    - Publicity & Advertising (5)
    - Sales/Reps (1)
    - Transport (2)
    - Despatch (3)

change order here please

Task 49

1/

CRUSING

by D. Armstrong

DS/ 2c/ Why is cruising so popular? There are many answers ~~to this question~~ but the simple ~~answer~~ one is that one can get the best of almost every holiday rolled into one – with the ~~exp~~ exception of isolation. stet

"A" 2c/ Perhaps the greatest number of people – & there are hundreds of thousands – prefer to cruise in or around the Mediterranean. They have the joy of going abroad without the troubles of tiring journeys, always an anticlimax on the return home; there are no language difficulties, the food is excellent,* the variety of companionship is unlimited, there are deck sports & there is always plenty of fun – or one can just laze in a deck chair,

m/ ~~travelling~~ either in a one-class ship or one which

m/ has ~~both~~ first class & tourist accommodation. "B"

Most people look forward to the 3 or 4 ports of call introducing them to countries which offer

places/ of/ wide varieties of scenery & historical interest. No-one visiting Gibraltar,‡ for instance would leave

vc/ without having seen the famous Barbary apes.

Palma ‡ is a paradise for those wishing to bathe in the clear warm sea in any of the many bays along the coast, or a coach or taxi ride will provide the sightseer with a variety of breath-taking beauty. (scenery of)

NP/ c/ [Barcelona tempts one to visit the shops with their magnificent window displays, the many

"B" though this is becoming rare.

* There are usually two sittings for each meal, 8.15 a.m., 12.30 p.m. & 7.00 p.m. or 9.00 a.m., 1.30 p.m. & 8.00 p.m.

‡ Passengers land by launch.

‡ There are frequent coach services between the ship & the town centre.

(continued)

Typist 2 pieces of work – both adverts for a magazine..

a) JOHN BURROUGHS & SONS – MARKET PLACE, PRESTON, PR1 2AC

- Biggest selection of Electrical Appliances in Town
- all at Discount Prices and Guaranteed

DISH WASHERS	VACUUM CLEANERS
ELECTRIC COOKERS REFRIGERATORS FREEZERS	WASHING MACHINES TUMBLE DRIERS SPIN DRIERS
RECONDITIONED APPLIANCES	
REPAIRS and SPARES	

– Free Delivery within our area

Call in & see our Showrooms
or
Send for our Catalogue

JOHN BORROUGHS & SONS (& address)
Please send me yr. catalogue
NAME
ADDRESS

---

b)

SUPRIMO

BUILT-IN AND CABINET FURNITURE
Invest for the Future
Take stock and check these features

65 mm
50 mm

BUILT-IN FURNITURE

- * Clean, straight lines f. elegance ③
- * Choice of wood ⑤
- * Easy to plan ①
- * Effective use of available space ②
- * Long mirrors indicate spaciousness ④
- * Interior fittings of drawers & shelves of highest quality ⑦
- * Bridging units to span beds &/or dressing-tables ⑥

CABINET FURNITURE

- * Beauty & strength of solid elm
- * Bevelled glass used throughout.
- * Craftsmanship unequalled in dovetailing & mitring
- * Versatile

MITRING

65 mm
37 mm

NOTE Both on A5 landscape

MONTJUICH

places recalling the vast historical background of the city, the replica of the Santa Maria in which Christopher Columbus sailed to America, & the fantastic illuminations at night, especially the fountains in the Parque de Montjuich which never fail to impress. These fountains change colour & shape every few minutes for a period of 3 hours during the tourist season.

AJACCIO

Corsica can be visited by landing at Calvi & joining a coach which travels along the narrow, tortuous mountain road on the W. coast, through uninhabited regions of majestic rugged beauty to the south, meeting other passengers who disembarked at Ajaccio,* where Napoleon was born. [Monastir* gives the uninitiated visitor a hot stony welcome, but within a few minutes one is surprised to discover a beautiful bay with fine sands & crystal clear water. Immediately behind this is a grand new hotel & not far away a modern theatre. This is a small historical town, with a new Kasbah & hospital. The progress & forward-looking programme of redevelopment is due to the zest of Habib Bourguiba, the President of Tunisia, who was born there.

Many women are still veiled, but they are now being encouraged to throw aside their safsari.

Palermo in Sicily has had such a turbulent past that not only has it beauty of scenery, but it is rich in literature & architecture, so that the one-day visitor feels he must return to see more of the treasures of this island, now a part of Italy.

* Passengers land by launch.

(continued)

THE CONFERENCE AGENCY

25 RUSSELL ROAD, BLACKPOOL, FY4 2AH

TELEPHONE 0253-007140

CONFERENCE RESERVATION FORM

I wish to make reservations as follows:

Mr./Mrs./Miss ______ Initials ______ Surnames (Block Capitals) ______

Name of society (Block Capitals) ____________________

Address (Block capitals) ____________________ POSTCODE __________

Telephone ____________________

ACCOMMODATION

Single room/s ☐ Double room/s ☐

MEALS

Full Board ☐ Half Board ☐ B/B ☐

ARRIVAL & DEPARTURES

Conference Dates: FROM ________ TO ________

Arrival on ____________ Morning/After-noon/Evening*

Departure on ____________ Before / after lunch*

I enclose cheque for £ NO. ____________

Date ________ Signature ____________

Position in Soc: ____________

*Delete as appropriate

Typist: Put double rooms first

Naples never fails to attract the sight-seer with its grandiose bay + the view of Mount (whilst) Vesuvius which dominates it. Near-by Pompeii lc/ is the best preserved specimen of a Roman town in existence. Naples is not only an interesting city in its own right, but it is a centre fr. which other towns may be visited. ~~Dom~~ By steamer, hovercraft or helicopter, one can cross to the Isle of Capri, which has a beauty + charm of its own. It has both historical + literary associations, + in more modern times it is here that Axel Munthe lived, the author ~~of~~ "The Story of San Michele". (Swedish doctor +) (who wrote)

There are an unlimited number of towns to be visited, each offering its own attractions in beauty, entertainment, customs + historical interest. If one wishes to go abroad in comfort, cruising is certainly one way of spending a very pleasant holiday.

"A" There are many different types of cruises, from the luxury liner crossing the Atlantic to the more modest, ~~but~~ very comfortable cargo boat, but . . . (though)

Task 58

Typist Please display so that the answers are inset + stand out clearly from the questions. abb. in full – + check for consistency. Questions in caps.

BIBLE QUIZ – WITH ANSWERS

1. Which was the first bird sent out of the ark?
   a raven. (Genesis viii, 7)

2. To what incident does 'The judgement of Solomon' refer?
   The two women quarrelling over a live + a dead baby. (I Kings iii, 16–28)

3. Who said, "Behold, I have heard that there is corn in Egypt?"
   Jacob. (Genesis xlii, 2)

4. Who said, "They that are whole need not a physician, but they that are sick", and why?
   Jesus.
   Because the scribes + Pharisees criticized him for eating with publicans. (Mark ii, 15–17)

5. What did the Good Samaritan do to render first aid? ~~the~~ of a man injured by robbers
   He bound ~~his~~ the wounds, pouring in oil + wine (Luke x, 34)

6. Who said, "Bring forth the best robe and put it on him ... + bring hither the fatted calf ... + let us eat + be merry ..." and why?
   The father of the prodigal son. [He was rejoicing that his son had returned home (Luke xv, 22–24).

7. Which 2 chapters in the Bible are identical?
   II Kings xix, + Isaiah xxxvii

8. Which verse contains twenty-five of the 26 letters of the English alphabet? — Ezra vii, 21

9. Which are the shortest verses in the Bible?
   In the O.T. – I Chronicles i, 25
   In the N.T. – John xi, 35.

10. How many books + chapters are there in the O.T.? In the N.T.? — In King James's version there are 39 books in the O.T. + 929 verses. [In the N.T. there are 27 books + 260 chapters.

The life and death of Cholmondeley *

By
Gerald M Durrell

Shortly before we left our hill-top hut at Bakebe and travelled down to our last camp at Kumba, we had a most unusual guest in the shape of Cholmondeley, Known to his friends as Chumley. [margin: to stay with us]

Chumley was a full-grown chimpanzee; his owner, a District Officer, was finding the ape's large size rather awkward, and he wanted to send him to ~~the~~ London Zoo as a present. [add A] He wrote asking us if we would mind taking Chumbley back with us when we left, and depositing him at his new home in London, and we replied that we would not mind at all.

I don't think ~~we~~ that either John or myself had the least idea how big Chumley was: I know that I visualized an ape of about three years old, standing about three feet high. I got a rude shock when Chumley moved in.

A so that he could visit the animal when he was back in England on leave.

* Taken from "The Overloaded Ark" published by Faber Faber

(continued)

Task 57

TYPIST. Please make a ~~draft~~ copy of the following - display as indicated, & leave a space of 4" x 3" for photograph. (PENCIL IN)

156 ASHTEAD ROAD, SEAFORD, EAST SUSSEX.

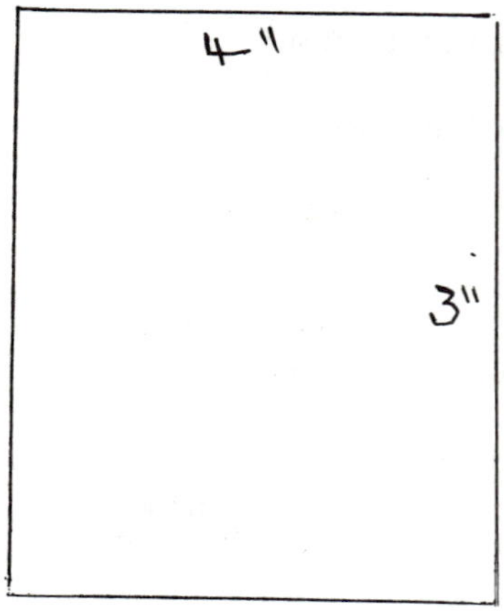

SITUATION - Enjoying a most convenient situation within a short distance of the Town Centre and Railway Station. The sea front is also readily accessible. Local shopping facilities are very close.

NP/ [An end of terrace SEMI-DETACHED HOUSE constructed of brick under a slate roof. Although requiring some modernisation and redecoration, the property has the unusual advantage of possible GARAGE SPACE, subject to the usual permissions being obtained.

Designed to provide compact ACCOMMODATION, arranged as follows:-

GROUND FLOOR

Small Entrance Hall

Lounge 12'9" x 11'6" with tiled fireplace & Relay T.V. point.

Dining Room. 14' 6" x 11'6" with cupboard understairs, fluorescent light and lighting point.

Kitchen - 11'6" x 5'9" of lean-to construction, fitted with single drainer sink unit (cold supply only) gas point. Door to BATHROOM with panelled bath. Door to Separate W.C.

FIRST FLOOR

Landing with lighting point.

Bedroom 1 12'6" x 11'9" with built-in wardrobe cupboard & storage cupboard over stairs.

Bedroom 2 11'6" x 7'10" with small built-in store cupboard.

Bedroom 3 7'9" x 6'6".

OUTSIDE

Small courtyard gardens to front & rear, Garden shed, fuel bunker. Possible GARAGE SPACE subject to the usual permissions being obtained.

RATEABLE VALUE: £370

PRICE £36,000 FREEHOLD.

seated sedately in a huge crate

He arrived ~~in a crate~~ in the back of a small van. When the doors of his crate were opened and Chumley stepped out with all the self-②confidence and ①ease of a film star, I was considerably shaken for, trs standing on his bow legs in a normal slouching chimp position, he came up to my waist, and if he had ~~stood up~~ straightened up, his head would have been level with my chest. He had ~~large~~ huge arms, and must have measured at least twice my measurements round his hairy chest. Owing to bad tooth growth both sides of his face were swollen out of all proportion, and this gave him a weird pugilistic look. His eyes were small, intelligent, and deep set; ~~to his~~ the top of his head was nearly bald owing to his habit of sitting and rubbing the palms of his hands backwards across his head Ⓐ This was no young chimp as I had expected, but a veteran of about eight or nine years old, fully mature, strong as a powerful man and, with considerable experience of life, to judge by his expression. Although he was not exactly a nice chimp

Ⓐ an exercise which seemed to afford him much pleasure and which he persisted in until the top of his skull was quite devoid of hair.

(continued)

Task 56

HOLLYDALE HOMES

Valley Road Bournemouth Hants BH3 5EJ

THE BEST THE SOUTH AND WEST CAN OFFER – (Centre)

EASTBOURNE

Colton Vale – in residential area near shops & school

9/ Houses from £45,950 Flats from £31,000

BOURNEMOUTH/POOLE

Harriett Close – in residential area on bus route to shops & station

Houses from £44,950 Bungalows fr. £40,500

LYME REGIS

Philip Avenue – on outskirts of town on bus route to shops & sea

Bungalows fr. £38,000

TORQUAY

Revill Drive – overlooking Babbacombe Downs close to sea & shops

Houses fr. £44,250 Bungalows fr. £40,000

ST. IVES

Clough Crescent – in residential area Close to sea & shops

Bungalows fr. £38,500

- -

Please send me details of your estates

at ____________________________

Name (Mr/Mrs/Miss) ____________________________

Address ____________________________

____

____

Typist: a) Draft copy please. b) Similar but with corner tear off. (Display may be altered) Omit prices but retain £ sign.

Hollydale Homes & address req required at top of tear off slip

to look at. he certainly had a terrific personality: it hit you as soon as you set eyes on him. His little eyes looked at you with a great intelligence, and there seemed to be a glitter of ironic laughter in their depths that made one feel uncomfortable. (I had seen more handsome).

He stood on the ground and surveyed his surroundings with a shrewd glance, and then he turned to me and held out one of his soft, pink-palmed hands to be shaken, with exactly that bored expression that one sees on the faces of professional hand-shakers. Round his neck was a thick chain, and its length drooped over the tailboard of the lorry. With an animal of less personality than Chumley, this would have been a sign of his subjugation, of his captivity. But Chumley wore ~~his~~ the chain with the superb air of a Lord Mayor; after shaking my hand so professionally, he turned and proceeded to pull the chain, out of his crate. He gathered it up carefully into loops, hung it over one hand and proceeded to walk into the hut as if he owned it.

and disappeared into the depths of his crate.

which measured some fifteen feet,

Typing of charts

First, there must be an understanding of the purpose of the chart in question, and an appreciation of the need for correct spacing to ensure easy reading. Secondly, it is necessary to use previously acquired expertise in display and in all forms of tabulation. Careful planning is of paramount importance, so that the whole is symmetrical and balanced, and perfectly clear.

Bar Charts and Pie Charts – *see* page 127

Note: Display work (other than that given in this section) will be found in the sections on The Entertainment World, Tabulation, Travel and Dinner Arrangements.

Task 55

Using the form below as a guide, type a form and instructions for the offer described below:

Our own home's special offer

Send today for our special Linen offer. Choose from the three items (obtainable in yellow, green or white) listed below, and complete the coupon. State the number of items required in the first column and the colour in the second column.

To order: Fill in the coupon in ink in block letters. Send with a crossed postal order or cheque (name and address on back please) payable to OUR OWN HOME Linen Offer, Charing Cross Road, London, WC2B 5PB

Set of 6 place mats	£8.05
Set of 6 table napkins	£7.75
Tablecloth	£9.80

CUT AROUND THE DOTTED LINE

I enclose PO/Cheque
to the value of £

Kitchenware offer

Set of 3 Saucepans with lids	£8.65
Non-stick Frypan	£5.38
Non-stick Milk pan	£4.25

State number of items required in appropriate box.
Each group counts as one item.
State colour (**Y**, **G** or **W**) in second column.

Name ....

Address ....

....

Town .... County ....

PLEASE USE BLOCK LETTERS

Name ....

Address ....

....

....

Thus, in the first
few minutes of arrival, Chumley had made us feel inferior
and had moved in, we felt, not because we wanted it,
but because he did. I almost felt I ought to apologise
for the mess on the table when he walked in.

He seated himself in a chair, dropped his chain on the
floor. It was quite obvious that he expected some sort of
refreshment after his tiring journey. I roared out to the
kitchen for them to make a cup of tea, for I had
been warned that Chumley had a great liking for
the cup that cheers. Leaving him sitting in the chair
I went out to his crate, and in it I found a tin plate
and a battered tin mug of colossal proportions.
When I returned to the hut bearing these Chumley
brightened considerably, and even went so far as to
praise me for my intelligence

"Ooooooo, umph!" he said, and then crossed his
legs and continued his inspection of the hut,

and then looked hopefully
at me.

and surveying our humble
abode with ill-concealed
disgust,

8 Display

Display is mainly a question of common sense, an eye for a pleasing appearance, and the application of the general rules of typewriting.

Displayed matter

This requires the ability to use centring, a variety of line spacing, capitalization and underscoring in the appropriate places, and a judicious use of justification in all its range of combinations, boxes (for enclosing words or sentences) and pointers (asterisks, dashes or heavy dots) to highlight items. It should be remembered that the importance of white spaces is to make the typewritten characters stand out. It is necessary to judge what effect each piece of work should have on the reader, what emphasis is needed, and which words should hold the attention or catch the eye.

Justifying

Very effective in a variety of ways for the display of advertisements, menus, programmes, etc. In continuous matter a draft is needed to assess the extra spaces required in each line so that it ends at the same point as the longest line.

Typing on lines

Remember that the characters should not touch the lines and every line of type should be the same distance above them.

Forms

Margins should be equal. All dotted or continuous lines should begin and end at definite positions, consistency being maintained, and at least one space should be left before and after any wording. Double spacing and sufficient lengths of line are needed for completion.

Tear-off slips

Horizontal: typing is as for forms, the 'slip' being centred both horizontally and vertically below the perforation, which is shown by hyphens or dashes typed from edge to edge across the paper.
Corner: For short line completion only. Plan from the bottom right-hand corner, and mark equidistant points on the base and side lines where required. Connect these with a light pencil line for easy alignment in the typewriter.

Decorative borders, etc

Decorations, fancy borders are tail pieces are sometimes needed, but care must be taken that work does not become too ornate. Wording for advertisements or invitations within the framework of an illustrative or pictorial outline can be effective.

Leaflets

All pages should be numbered/marked in pencil to avoid confusion when in the typewriter, and a backing sheet is needed between the sheets if typing on the folded leaflet. Margins need care on inside pages to ensure a pleasing appearance.

Six-page leaflets

With a sheet of A4 paper, portrait, beginning at the bottom, fold over twice to give three equal sections. Turn over with the left hand and twist, so that the folded edge is on the left and the opening is on the right. The front page is now on top. Mark this F/P. Open up and number the three inside pages and the remaining two outer pages.

Charts

These give pictorial accounts of businesses, their stocks, profits, structures, etc., and are commonly used in offices to obtain on-the-spot recognition of a particular situation, each one requiring the chart most suited to its own needs, to indicate the 'story' which is to be told.

Organization charts

These indicate the structure of the organization, the level of responsibility and the relationship between each, and the functions of the staff involved. They can be prepared in horizontal (Task 71) or vertical form (Task 61).

Flow charts

These indicate the 'flow' or chain of procedures in any given operation. They are frequently used in analysing and decision making. The variety of shaped symbols, representing different procedures, are generally reproduced by hand, using a special 'template' (shapes cut in a plastic frame) to ensure uniformity of size. Lines, broken lines and arrows all assist in following the progress of the procedures.

THE EARLY DAYS OF SKI-ING IN SWITZERLAND

When winter sports are enjoyed by so many, it is
difficult to realise that the ski was only introduced into
Switzerland ~~in the late~~ at the end of the 19th century. Here is
stet the ~~story~~ account as told by Madame Quincle, one of the first skiers.
(QUINCHE)
In 1889 a Jura Bern~~ois~~ese schoolmaster returned home
after several years' absence, bringing with him a pair of
skis he had used in Norway. Working in the town, he
no longer needed them, so he decided to sell them, but
no-one was interested. The following summer he heard
that a young vicar from Neuchatel, Herman Quincle,
(married to an English lady) had arrived to take over a neighbouring parish. It
might/ was suggested that the skis ~~may~~ be of use to him. "A"
The vicar agreed and, after only one lesson – on his lawn
⊙ in August – he set about finding a second pair for his wife.
proved This ~~which~~ was no easy task as skis were unknown in
uc/⊙ Switzerland, ~~so~~ an application was sent to Stockholm
NP/ T, after 7 months, the skis arrived. [Although it
was spring, a cold spell enabled the vicar & his
trs. wife to make their debut on 2 ft of snow.

That winter was very cold & at the end of
October the skis were brought out. It then became
s/ a common sight to see the vicar & his wife practising
lc/ on the slopes in front of the Vicarage, much to the
great amusement of the villagers who watched them from
their doorways & discreetly disappeared when one
or the other had a spill. Learning was not an easy
~~matter~~ as the skis were very primitive, having only a
(without any clasps) piece of leather for the tip of the foot & a circular
piece of reed in a leather holder round the heel. "B"
Without instruction or any indication as to
(Correct) their use, they had to learn by experience.

One afternoon in mid-winter the vicar was
called to the bed-side of a sick man & he left

(continued)

Task 53

WINTER

When icicles hang by the wall
And Dick the shepherd blows his nail,
And Tom bears logs into the hall,
And milk comes frozen home in pail;
When blood is nipt, and ways be foul,
Then nightly sings the staring owl
Tuwhoo!
Tuwhit! tuwhoo! A merry note!
While greasy Joan doth keel the pot.

When all around the wind doth blow,
And coughing drowns the parson's saw,
And birds sit brooding in the snow,
And Marion's nose looks red & raw;
When roasted crabs hiss in the bowl —
Then nightly sings the staring owl
Tuwhoo!
Tuwhit! tuwhoo! A merry note!
While greasy Joan doth keel the pot.

— W. Shakespeare

Typist
Indents seem non-existent in the second verse — will you insert them please.

Task 54

THE NOBLE NATURE

It is not growing like a tree
In bulk, doth make Man better be;
Or standing long an oak, three hundred year,
To fall a log at last, dry, bald and sere;
SERE
A lily of a day
Is fairer far in May,
Although it fall and die that night —
It was the plant and flower of light u.c.
In small proportions we just beauties see;
And in short measures life may perfect be.

— B. Johnson

for the outlying village on his skis. He was kept longer
⊙ of than he had ~~anticipated~~ expected & started ~~for home~~ for home after dark, ~~but~~
v.c. the falling snow had obliterated ~~his marks~~ the trail of his skis & soon
NP he realised he was lost. [Meanwhile, there was great
⁷/ anxiety at the vicarage, & after much consultation among
the parishoners it was decided that the church bells
should be sounded.

run on (For 2 hours the church bells rang out through the
darkness across the mountains, at first frightening, & then
arousing the curiosity of all the neighbouring villages. It
was not until ten o'clock that the vicar arrived back,
exhausted, having been guided by the sound of the bells.
The next day, & for some time ~~to come~~ after, the story of the
⁷/v.c. vicars "Planchettes" was the general topic of conversation.

examine Their curiosity aroused, several young men (sons of the doctor & the lawyer) went up to the
village to ~~investigate~~ the skis which had created such a
sensation, & subsequently an order for four more pairs
NP was sent to Stockholm. [The following winter six pairs
of skis glided down the slopes of the Jura mountains, &
in 1892 a party of 6 skiers crossed the Chasseral to
descend into the Valley of Saint-Imier. Later that year
another pair was taken to Montreux, but it was not
for some time that skis could be bought in the
Para. Country. [One of the two original pairs of skis was still
in existence at Lausanne until 1938, when an over-
energetic gardener, not realising their historical value,
⊂ broke them up for fire-wood.

"A" on his long treks from one village to another.

"B" At the slightest false move, the ski would
slip from the foot.

Task 52

DEATH THE LEVELLER.

The glories of our blood and state
Are shadows, not substantial things;
There is no armour against fate;
Death lays his icy hand on kings:
Sceptre and Crown
Must tumble down,
And in the dust be equal made
With the poor crooked scythe and spade.

Some men with swords may reap the field.
And plant fresh laurels where they kill:
But their strong nerves at last must yield;
They tame but one another still:
Early or late
They stoop to fate,
And must give up their murmuring breath
When they, pale captives, creep to death.

The garlands wither on your brow;
Then boast no more your mighty deeds;
Upon Death's purple altar now
See where the victor-victim bleeds:
Your heads must come
To the cold tomb;
Only the actions of the just
Smell sweet, and blossom in their dust.

- J. Shirley